THE ILLUSTRATED GUIDE TO
VISIBLE LEARNING

THE ILLUSTRATED GUIDE TO
VISIBLE LEARNING

An Introduction to What Works Best in Schools

JOHN HATTIE | DOUGLAS FISHER
NANCY FREY | JOHN ALMARODE
ILLUSTRATIONS BY **TARYL HANSEN**

CORWIN
A Sage Company

FOR INFORMATION:

Corwin

A Sage Company

2455 Teller Road

Thousand Oaks, California 91320

(800) 233-9936

www.corwin.com

Sage Publications Ltd.

1 Oliver's Yard

55 City Road

London EC1Y 1SP

United Kingdom

Sage Publications India Pvt. Ltd.

Unit No 323-333, Third Floor, F-Block

International Trade Tower Nehru Place

New Delhi 110 019

India

Sage Publications Asia-Pacific Pte. Ltd.

18 Cross Street #10-10/11/12

China Square Central

Singapore 048423

Vice President and Editorial
  Director: Monica Eckman

Director and Publisher: Lisa Luedeke

Content Development Editor: Sarah Ross

Product Associate: Zachary Vann

Production Editor: Laura Barrett

Typesetter: C&M Digitals (P) Ltd.

Proofreader: Caryne Brown

Indexer: Integra

Cover and Interior Designer: Gail Buschman

Marketing Manager: Megan Naidl

Printed in the United States of America

Library of Congress Control Number: 2024936090

ISBN 978-1-0719-5309-9

This book is printed on acid-free paper.

24 25 26 27 28 10 9 8 7 6 5 4

CONTENTS

VL SIGNATURE PRACTICE #10: IMPLEMENTATION 109

VL SIGNATURE PRACTICE #11: EVALUATIVE THINKING 121

Note From the Publisher: The authors have provided content that is available to you through a QR (quick response) code. To read a QR code, you must have a smartphone or tablet with a camera. We recommend that you download a QR code reader app that is made specifically for your phone or tablet brand.

Content may also be accessed at **www.visiblelearningmetax.com**

ABOUT THE AUTHORS

John Hattie is an award-winning education researcher and best-selling author with nearly 30 years of experience examining what works best in student learning and achievement. His research, better known as Visible Learning, is a culmination of nearly 30 years synthesizing more than 2,100 meta-analyses comprising more than 100,000 studies involving over 300 million students around the world. He has presented and keynoted in over 350 international conferences and has received numerous recognitions for his contributions to education. His notable publications include *Visible Learning*, *Visible Learning for Teachers*, *Visible Learning and the Science of How We Learn*, *Visible Learning for Mathematics, Grades K-12*, and, most recently, *10 Mindframes for Visible Learning*.

Douglas Fisher is professor and chair of educational leadership at San Diego State University and a teacher leader at Health Sciences High and Middle College. Previously, Doug was an early intervention teacher and elementary school educator. He is the recipient of an International Reading Association William S. Grey citation of merit and an Exemplary Leader award from the Conference on English Leadership of NCTE, as well as a Christa McAuliffe award for excellence in teacher education. In 2022, he was inducted into the Reading Hall of Fame by the Literacy Research Association. He has published numerous articles on reading and literacy, differentiated instruction, and curriculum design, as well as books such as *The Teacher Clarity Playbook*, *PLC+*, *Visible Learning for Literacy*, *Comprehension: The Skill, Will, and Thrill of Reading*, *How Feedback Works*, *Teaching Reading* and most recently, *Teaching Students to Drive their Learning*.

Nancy Frey is a professor in educational leadership at San Diego State University and a teacher leader at Health Sciences High and Middle College. She is a member of the International Literacy Association's Literacy Research Panel. Her published titles include *Visible Learning for Literacy*, *The Vocabulary Playbook*, *Removing Labels*, *Rebound*, *The Social-Emotional Learning Playbook*, and *How Scaffolding Works*. Nancy is a credentialed special educator, reading specialist, and administrator in California and learns from teachers and students every day.

John Almarode is a bestselling author and has worked with schools, classrooms, and teachers all over the world on the translation and application of the science of learning to the classroom, school, and home environments, and what works best in teaching and learning. He has done so in Australia, Canada, Egypt, England, Qatar, Saudi Arabia, Scotland, South Korea, Thailand and all across the United States. He is an Associate Professor of Education in the College of Education. In 2015, John was awarded the inaugural Sarah Miller Luck Endowed Professorship. In 2021, John was honored with an Outstanding Faculty Award from the State Council for Higher Education in Virginia. Continuing his collaborative work with colleagues on what works best in teaching and learning, *How Tutoring Works*, *Visible Learning in Early Childhood*, and *How Learning Works*, all with Corwin Press, were released in 2021.

ABOUT THE ILLUSTRATOR

Taryl Hansen, illustrator, is a National Board Certified teacher, associate trainer of Cognitive Coaching[SM], a highly skilled visual practitioner, and the founder of Frame the Message Ink. As a live graphic recorder, Taryl works internationally to create vibrant and engaging visuals that bring essential elements to the forefront for learners, enhancing retention and engagement, and inspiring learners to collaborate in more meaningful ways.

WELCOME!

This book is about learning. We are about learning. We want to make learning visible for students, their caregivers, teachers, and leaders. Learning should be seen and experienced. Educators should regularly talk about learning and what it means to learn.

Together, we have decades of experience with teaching and learning. Experience is a valuable teacher, but an incomplete one. We need evidence. We need to collect, interpret, and use evidence to make optimal decisions with and for students. In this book, we draw on published evidence that has the greatest potential to accelerate students' learning. Note that we said potential. That's because ideas must be implemented, and implementation is one of the great challenges in schools. We need to "know thy impact." When ideas from research are implemented with sufficient frequency, intensity, and duration, the likelihood of impact increases.

And that's what Visible Learning really means. It means having an impact on the learning lives of students, one that can be evaluated and monitored. Our goal is to have an impact on you—the educators. To make the foundational ideas of Visible Learning® accessible to you, such that your ability to implement those ideas is increased.

BIG DATA

There are thousands and thousands of studies published every year. It's really hard to keep up and know what works best to ensure that students learn more and better each year—particularly when most influences show a positive effect on learning and achievement. The Visible Learning database is possibly the largest collection of educational research ever assembled and is designed to help educators and families make sense of these studies.

To do so, statisticians developed a tool to aggregate and combine studies to see the overall, average impact of the research. This tool is known as a **meta-analysis,** and the numerical average is called an **effect size**.

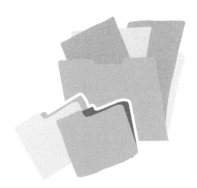

Meta-analyses are collections of studies on the same topic. The author of the meta-analysis standardizes the effects so that the various studies can be compared and combined.

An **effect size** tells us how powerful a given influence is on the outcome. Effect sizes can be negative or positive and can be small, medium, or large. The larger the number, the more likely it is to influence the outcome.

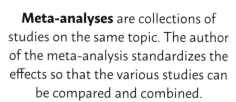

Individual meta-analyses, often written by different research teams, can be themselves combined to determine the average effect size of a given influence. In doing so, more and more data are integrated, and the number of studies, students, and influences increases. Questions about the impact of many factors can also be explored (e.g., country of study, curricula domain, age of student, and so much more).

Visible Learning is a collection of meta-analyses where the outcome is academic achievement and learning. There are thousands of meta-analyses in the research that represent hundreds of millions of students. The collection continues to grow every year. In fact, after the publication of this illustrated guide, the publishing of meta-analyses will continue, and our knowledge and understanding of teaching and learning will continue to grow. Thus, we want to make sure you have access to the latest findings.

Effect sizes for **over 350 different influences** on learning have been calculated and shared on the Meta[X] database. These are available at **www.visiblelearningmetax.com** and will reflect the most recent evidence available.

Visible Learning Meta[X]
qrs.ly/1xfph0f

This is the **effect size thermometer**, which you will see often throughout this book. It shows the relative size of the influence. If it is located in the **red zone**, it is an *above average effect* and worth noting. In the **yellow zone**, it is *above zero* (it positvely impacts achievement) *but below average.* If in the **blue zone**, it has a *negative impact on achievement.*

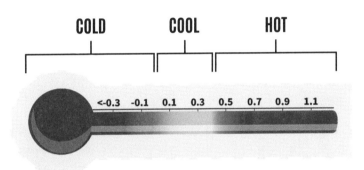

But one thing has remained constant over the years of collecting this meta-analytic data: **the average influence of all of the things we do in school is about 0.40.**

Thus, **effect sizes over 0.40** are above average and have the greatest potential to improve learning outcomes for students.

Our fascination is this:
What are the underlying factors that result in something being above versus below average?

NOT EVERYTHING WORKS

One big idea generated from the Visible Learning database is that some things simply work better than others. Not everything that we do in schools is useful and worth the effort. In fact, a few things that happen in schools have a negative impact on learning.

Some influences are fairly obvious. When teachers and schools **decrease disruptive behavior**, students learn more. **The effect size is 0.82.** Again, probably not a surprise.

On the other end, when students miss school, they learn less. We did not need big data to tell us that. **The effect size of attendance is -0.46.** It has a negative impact on learning.

Lectures also have a negative impact on learning with an effect size of -0.35. When students are placed in a passive position for long periods of time, they learn less.

Recognizing what does not work helps educators consider what might work best to improve student learning. Some of the influences that have a negative impact on learning include:

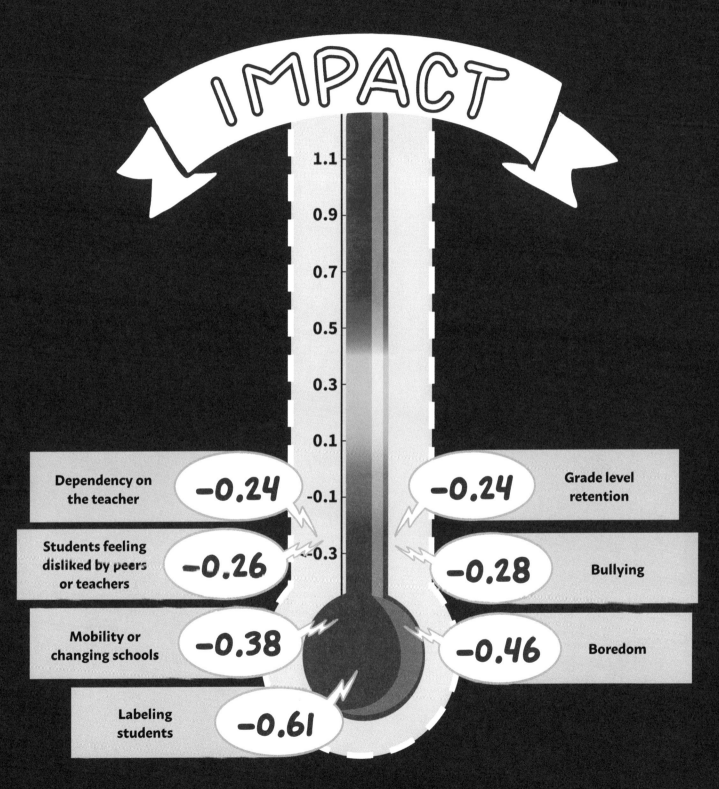

MAKING A LIST . . .

As the American journalist and humorist H. Allen Smith noted, the human animal differs from the lesser primates in its passion for lists. We could make a list of all the influences and rank them by their overall effect. We could take *The Late Show* approach and create the top-10 list and revise it each time the numbers change. But we won't.

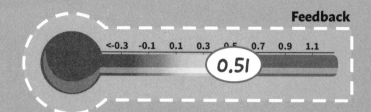

Feedback

| <-0.3 | -0.1 | 0.1 | 0.3 | 0.5 | 0.7 | 0.9 | 1.1 |

0.51

Lists can mask the complexities and nuances of the data.

There are some effect sizes that can be deceiving. At first glance, the low effect size may give the false impression that it does not work or is somehow less important than others.

Consider the effect size for feedback, 0.51. The fact that this particular influence has an above-average potential to accelerate learning should come as no surprise to any of us in the classroom. We all know and believe that feedback is important. But one-third of feedback can be negative, so there is a deeper story to tell about feedback.

Note-taking

| <-0.3 | -0.1 | 0.1 | 0.3 | 0.5 | 0.7 | 0.9 | 1.1 |

0.33

Note-taking has an effect size of 0.33, below the overall average in terms of its impact. But it's fairly easy to implement and has a reasonable impact, so why not teach students to take notes? Importantly, the effect size reflects the research that has been conducted and can point out what needs to be done to increase the effect.

For example, note-taking for students who simply copy their teacher's notes has **little impact on learning**.

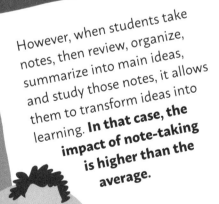

However, when students take notes, then review, organize, summarize into main ideas, and study those notes, it allows them to transform ideas into learning. **In that case, the impact of note-taking is higher than the average.**

Well-being

| <-0.3 | -0.1 | 0.1 | 0.3 | 0.5 | 0.7 | 0.9 | 1.1 |

0.24

Look at the effect size for well-being, 0.24. This is below average, right? We might walk away from this effect size believing that somehow a student's sense of well-being is not that important. This would be an incorrect and dangerous interpretation.

Instead, we must consider the complex nature of our schools and classrooms. For example, a student's sense of well-being correlates with a capacity to receive and integrate feedback. Well-being is foundational for other aspects of teaching and learning. Thus, focusing solely on the effect size is overlooking the important and valuable aspects of the teaching and learning environment. **A rank order or list is not the way to approach Visible Learning.**

If we just made a "best of" list, note-taking may not make it to the factors that are considered for *implementation*.

But when integrated into an instructional model focused on learning, note-taking likely would make the cut.

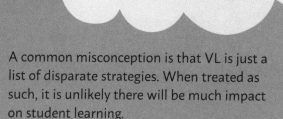

A common misconception is that VL is just a list of disparate strategies. When treated as such, it is unlikely there will be much impact on student learning.

But when implemented cohesively, influences rise in impact.

In this book, we demonstrate how Visible Learning evidence can be cohesively integrated into key messages, mindframes, and models that allow for implementation, taking the research from concept to classroom.[1]

BIG IDEAS

Visible learning uses evidence to tell a story. There are four big ideas in the story that tie the research together. These big ideas are explored in more detail in the sections that follow.

BIG IDEA #1: CLIMATE FIRST, LEARNING SECOND, ACHIEVEMENT THIRD.

- **Foster a learning community:** Teachers and school leaders should create and sustain an environment where learning flourishes for all students.

- **Develop social, emotional, and academic skills:** Teachers and school leaders should create a positive and inviting learning environment that fosters, nurtures, and sustains a strong sense of belonging and well-being.

- **Maintain high expectations for all students:** Teachers and school leaders should seek to leverage the potential of every student and demonstrate their belief in this potential through high expectations for growth and learning.

BIG IDEA #2: STUDENTS SHOULD DRIVE THEIR LEARNING.

- **Advance different types of knowledge:** Teachers should strive to teach not only factual knowledge but also problem-solving skills and the ability to apply knowledge in various contexts.

- **Teach learning strategies:** Teachers should equip students with effective learning strategies, enabling them to make progress and overcome challenges independently.

- **Accelerate and release teacher responsibility:** Teachers should know how to effectively guide and support students in their learning journey, gradually empowering them to take more ownership of their learning.

- **Cultivate self-driving learners:** Students should become active participants in their own learning, developing skills such as self-assessment, planning, seeking feedback, monitoring, and evaluating their progress.

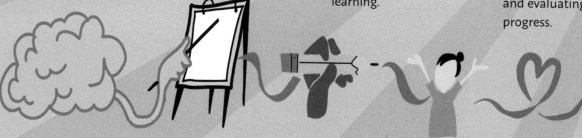

BIG IDEA #3: KNOW THY IMPACT.

- **Strengthen evaluative thinking:** Teachers, school leaders, and students should learn to think critically, assess credibility, make informed choices, ask probing questions, and distinguish right from wrong.

- **Demonstrate impact:** Teachers and leaders should be skilled at assessing and evaluating their own effectiveness based on evidence, using this information to improve their teaching.

- **Improve the system:** System leaders should focus on identifying successful practices, scaling them up across schools, and reducing unnecessary workload, while recognizing and valuing the impact of educators.

tells a STORY!

BIG IDEA #4: COLLECTIVE RESPONSIBILITY FOR LEARNING.

- **Create the collective.** Teachers, school leaders, and students should create and maintain individual and collective efficacy.

- **Focus on skills.** Teachers, school leaders, and students continuously focus on the *I* and *We* skills necessary to ensure collaborations are productive.

- **Take ownership.** Teachers, school leaders, and students should assume responsibility for their own learning and the learning of others.

MINDFRAMES

When it comes to impacting students' learning, it's less about what educators do and more about how we think about what we do. Educators' ways of thinking or mindsets, beliefs, and attitudes significantly influence the quality of education students receive. Visible Learning focuses on specific mindframes that influence how students, teachers, families, and leaders think. You can use these as a self-assessment tool, identify areas of strength, and plan on your own where to go next.

LEARNERS

I am confident that I can learn.

I set, implement, and monitor an appropriate mix of achieving and deep learning goals.

I strive to improve and enjoy my learning.

I strive to master and acquire surface and deep learning.

I work to contribute to a positive learning culture.

I know multiple learning strategies and know how best to use them.

I have the confidence and skills to learn from and contribute to group learning.

I can hear, understand, and action feedback.

I can evaluate my learning.

I am my own teacher.

TEACHERS

I am an evaluator of my impact on student learning.

I see assessment as informing my impact and next steps.

I collaborate with my peers and my students about my conceptions of progress and my impact.

I am a change agent and believe all students can improve.

I strive for challenge and not merely "doing my best."

I give and help students understand feedback, and I interpret and act on feedback given to me.

I engage as much in dialogue as in monologue.

I explicitly inform students what successful impact looks like from the outset.

I build relationships and trust so that learning can occur in a place where it is safe to make mistakes and learn from others.

I focus on learning and the language of learning.

LEADERS

I am an evaluator of my impact.

I see assessment as feedback to me.

I collaborate regarding my conceptions of progress and my progress.

I am a change agent.

I strive to challenge.

I give and help teachers understand feedback.

I engage as much in dialogue as monologue.

I explicitly inform teachers what successful impact looks like.

I build relationships and trust.

I focus on the language of learning.

FAMILY/CAREGIVER

I have appropriately high expectations.

I make reasonable demands and am highly responsive to my child.

I am not alone.

I develop my child's skill, will, and sense of thrill.

I love learning.

I know the power of feedback, and that success thrives on errors.

I am a parent, not a teacher.

I expose my child to language, language, language.

I appreciate that my child is not perfect, nor am I.

I am an evaluator of my impact.

BELONGING, IDENTITIES, AND EQUITY[2]

We strive to invite all to learn.

We value engagement in learning.

We collaborate to learn and thrive.

We cultivate fortifying and sustaining environments for all identities.

We acknowledge, affirm, and embrace the identities of all our students.

We remove barriers to students' learning, including barriers related to identities.

We discover, correct, and disrupt inequities.

We embrace diverse cultures and identities.

We recognize and disrupt biases.

We create equitable opportunities and eliminate barriers to opportunities.

VL Signature Practice #1:
CLASSROOM AND SCHOOL CLIMATE

CLASSROOM AND SCHOOL CLIMATE

School climate starts with expectations. We tend to get what we expect. When we expect greatness, we are more likely to achieve it. And when we expect mediocrity, we are spectacularly effective in realizing low levels of learning.

Teachers with high expectations believe ALL their students will grow exceptionally, not simply make "normal" progress. A core notion is that teachers who have high (or low) expectations tend to have this for ALL students.

High-expectation teachers do the following:[3]

- Undertake diagnosis to determine what students already know and can do, and what challenges in their learning they need next

- Communicate learning intentions and success criteria with the class

- Ask more open questions, designed to extend or enhance students' thinking by requiring them to think more deeply

- Invite students to ask questions about their work they are not sure about

- Manage behavior positively and proactively

- Make more positive statements and create a high-trust class climate where errors are seen as opportunities not embarrassments

- Take a facilitative role and support students to make choices about their learning

- Link achievement to motivation, effort, and goal setting

- Teach the skills students need to work alone and with a variety of peers for positive peer modeling

- Provide less grouping by ability and allow all learners to engage in advanced activities

- Undertake more assessment and monitoring so that their teaching strategies can be adjusted when necessary

- Respond to incorrect answers by exploring the wrong answer, rephrasing explanations, or scaffolding the student to the correct answer

- Give specific, instructional feedback about students' achievement in relation to learning goals and where to move next in teaching and learning

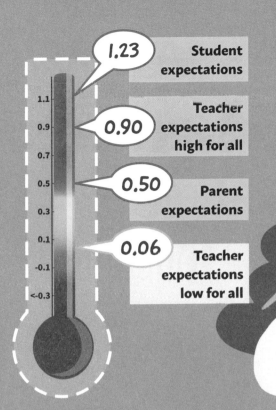

1.23 Student expectations

0.90 Teacher expectations high for all

0.50 Parent expectations

0.06 Teacher expectations low for all

Teachers need to have high expectations and stretch goals for all students regardless of their prior ability, race/ethnicity, disability status, social class, or gender identity.

Teachers with lower expectations assign tasks that are less cognitively demanding, spend time repeating information, focus on classroom rules and procedures, and accept a lower standard of work.

When teachers believe that students are low-achieving students[4] **they**

LOW EXPECTATIONS

- Are criticized more often for failure
- Receive less feedback
- Are called on less often
- Have less eye contact with the teacher
- Have fewer friendly interactions with the teacher
- Experience acceptance of their ideas less often

All students can accelerate their learning, although there may be different paths and times to succeed.

SCHOOL CLIMATE FACILITATES BELONGING

"Belonging is the feeling that we're part of a larger group that values, respects, and cares for us—and to which we feel we have something to contribute."[5] Students learn more when they feel that they belong in their classrooms and school. **Belonging's effect on learning is 0.46.** In addition, when educators feel they belong to the school, they perform better and students learn more. There are several dimensions of belonging[6] that can be fostered in schools.

WELCOMED

How we are greeted each time we meet signals importance and fosters belonging.

Indicators for Students
- Greeting students
- Showing enthusiasm for students' return to class

Indicators for Staff
- Greeting colleagues
- Asking authentic questions
- Engaging in authentic conversations

INVITED

The ways people are invited signals their value and fosters a sense of belonging.

Indicators for Students
- Asking peers to play and dialogue
- Extending invitations for extracurricular events and clubs
- Modeling inviting behavior

Indicators for Staff
- Sending invites for meetings and learning events
- Extending invitations for other professional opportunities (advising, club sponsorship)

PRESENT

Who is in attendance and actually present.

Indicators for Students
- Strong student attendance rates
- Participating in class activities

Indicators for Staff
- Strong staff attendance rates
- Participating in team meetings and learning activities

KNOWN

The depth to which we know others.

Indicators for Students
- Pronouncing names correctly
- Strong teacher-student relationships
- Focusing on strengths

Indicators for Staff
- Addressing biased and stereotyped language
- Emotional intelligence and positive dialogues

ACCEPTED
Ways we are recognized and celebrated as a member of the group.

Indicators for Students
- Positive body language and nonverbal messages
- Symbols of respect for all student groups
- Culturally sustaining instructional materials

Indicators for Staff
- Positive body language and nonverbal messages
- Inclusive beliefs and actions about students, staff, and community

LOVED

When it comes to school, we're talking about the selfless, unconditional love that conveys compassion and empathy.

Indicators for Students
- Providing comfort
- Showing patience, effort, and unity
- Building meaningful relationships

Indicators for Staff
- Making statements of empathy
- Using words of grace and forgiveness

NEEDED

We know that our contributions are valued because others rely on us for consequential work.

Indicators for Students
- Helping each other
- Peer tutoring
- Collaborating with peers

Indicators for Staff
- Peer coaching
- Peer-to-peer conversations
- Sharing resources and ideas

BEFRIENDED

Being friendly and encouraging and facilitating friendships.

Indicators for Students
- Structured opportunities for students to interact with a wide range of peers
- Integrated peer relationship development in the curriculum

Indicators for Staff
- Social opportunities for staff to interact
- Collegial and friendly interactions in hallways, restrooms, and classrooms

SUPPORTED

Recognition of our uniqueness, and systems to aid our participation.

Indicators for Students
- Strong instructional scaffolds in place
- Sophisticated tiers of support
- Modeling and demonstrating, not just telling information

Indicators for Staff
- Professional learning is practical and responsive to staff needs and interests
- Peer coaching and feedback
- Restorative conversations

HEARD

Active listening to others sends a message that they are valued and have ideas worth considering.

Indicators for Students
- Active listening (and teachers talking less)
- Soliciting feedback from students
- Student choice and decision-making in how they demonstrate understanding

Indicators for Staff
- Staff involvement in decisions
- Distributed leadership
- Leaders engaged in dialogue, not monologue

INVOLVED

We participate in the tasks and workflow of the group.

Indicators for Students
- Opportunities for collaborative learning
- Using academic language
- Students setting goals for their learning

Indicators for Staff
- Collaborating with colleagues in team meetings
- Contributing to tasks required to operate the school

SCHOOL CLIMATE FOSTERS CLASSROOM COHESION AND FRIENDSHIPS

In great classrooms, students cooperate and collaborate to reach common goals. They describe the environment as friendly and supportive, and there are classroom agreements and systems in place to ensure that a respectful environment is maintained. In these classrooms, students tend to learn more.

Members of cohesive groups tend to have several characteristics.[7] They

- have a collective identity

- experience a bond and a desire to remain part of the group

- share a sense of purpose, working together on a meaningful task

- establish a structured pattern of communication

- provide opportunities for students to sit with and interact with different peers on a regular basis

- structure collaborative tasks with individual accountability and opportunities for success

- encourage and reward student cooperation

- model friendly and supportive behavior for students

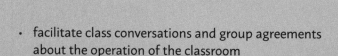

- facilitate class conversations and group agreements about the operation of the classroom

- teach procedures for routine tasks, such as entering the room, submitting work, gaining attention, and requesting support

- spend class time focused on group goals

- balance cooperation with competitions, dividing the class into groups and having them compete as groups in academic tasks

- allow students to vote on aspects of the classroom such as layout, discussion topics, reading materials, jobs, or rewards

Cohesion is also built and reinforced when groups of students have shared experiences and opportunities to recall and reflect on those experiences.

Shared experiences, from field trips to lab experiments to books read together, remind students that they belong, are not alone, and function as a group. These shared experiences reinforce the idea that the members of the group are connected to one another in meaningful ways.

| <-0.3 | -0.1 | 0.1 | 0.3 | 0.5 | 0.7 | 0.9 | 1.1 |

0.35

Friendships

0.66

Classroom cohesion

Remember our conversation about well-being?

Classroom cohesion and friendships should aim to promote a sense of well-being. A sense of well-being is foundational to learning.

SCHOOL CLIMATE INCLUDES TEACHER RELATIONSHIPS AND TEACHER SUPPORT

At the most basic level, we all want to be liked. And we perform better when we have strong relationships with those teaching us. Healthy, growth-producing relationships help students learn; when they see their teachers as supportive, they learn more. In a phrase, these teachers are warm demanders who expect that students treat the teacher and their peers respectfully and that they participate in the academic tasks assigned to them.[8] Warm demanders approach students, including students with problematic behavior, with unconditional positive regard,[9] a genuine caring despite what that student might do or say.

High-impact teachers balance relationships and support, are warm demanders, and implement invitational teaching. This involves:[10]

OPTIMISM

the potential of each classroom member is untapped, and every classroom member is responsible for finding ways to help others exceed what they think is their potential. Teachers are important in creating optimistic learning environments, and so are students. In an inviting classroom, students support the learning of their peers and understand that they are key in one other's learning

TRUST

the ongoing relationships between the teacher and students. In trusting classrooms, teachers and students assume positive intentions, and seek to build, maintain, and repair those relationships

INTENTIONAL

RESPECT

actions are fostered that communicate an understanding of everyone's autonomy, identity, and value to the learning community. Shared responsibility is crucial, and members of the classroom, including the teacher, see themselves as stewards for maintaining the social and emotional well-being of others

<-0.3 -0.1   0.1   0.3   0.5   0.7   0.9   1.1

Teacher-student support 0.32

0.62 **Teacher-student relations**

INVITING

INTENTIONALITY

an invitation to learning means that the practices, policies, processes, and programs of classrooms and schools are carefully designed to convey trust, respect, and optimism to all

PURPOSE

high-trust environments are built to encourage students to safely encounter challenges to their learning, make and learn from mistakes, see errors as opportunities not embarrassments, and learn from their peers

Source: Purkey & Novak (1996).

When intentionality and invitation are combined, there are four possible types of teachers:[11]

Intentionally uninviting teachers . . .	**Intentionally inviting teachers . . .**
• Are judgmental and belittling • Display little care or regard • Are uninterested in the lives and feelings of students • Isolate themselves from school life • Seek power over students	• Are consistent and steady with students • Notice learning and struggle • Respond regularly with feedback • Seek to build, maintain, and repair relationships
Unintentionally uninviting teachers . . .	**Unintentionally inviting teachers . . .**
• Distance themselves from students • Have low expectations • Don't feel effective, and blame students for shortcomings • Fail to notice student learning or struggle • Offer little feedback to learners	• Are eager but unreflective • Are energetic but rigid when facing problems • Are unaware of what works in their practice and why • Have fewer means for responding when student learning is resistant to their usual methods

VL Signature Practice #2:

TEACHER CLARITY

VL SIGNATURE PRACTICE #2

TEACHER CLARITY

When teachers are clear in their expectations and instruction, students learn more.

Teacher clarity is both a method and a mindset. It's teaching that is organized, intentional, and based on transparent expectations. When educators are clear, students can better plan, predict, set goals, and judge their own progress.

Teacher clarity is an umbrella term that describes the crucial dimensions of teaching effectiveness, each with an effect size above the average:

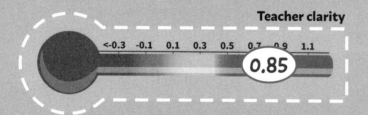

Teacher clarity

<-0.3 -0.1 0.1 0.3 0.5 0.7 0.9 1.1

0.85

Organization of instruction such that knowledge is built systematically, logically, and intentionally

(ES = 0.64)

Explaining content in ways that are accurate and developmentally appropriate

(ES = 0.70)

Providing examples and guided practice that illuminate application, highlight errors to avoid, and allow students to take on the learning using scaffolds as needed

(ES = 0.46)

Each of these elements must align with what students are expected to learn and how they will know that they have learned it. These are the learning intentions and success criteria. But remember, teacher clarity is more than learning intentions and success criteria.

TC > LI + SC

Learning intentions and success criteria are critical aspects of teacher clarity and visible learning. These transparent expectations invite students into learning and help ensure that the lessons are logical and organized.

When lessons are clear, students can answer these three questions:

1. **What am I learning today?**

2. **Why am I learning this?**

3. **How will I know that I learned it?**

Interpretations based on assessment of student learning such that teachers make informed decisions about what's next, and students understand their own progress

(ES = 0.64)

Ensure students understand the criteria of success, when good is good enough, and when the goals are appropriately challenging

(ES = 0.88)

WHAT AM I LEARNING TODAY?

This is the learning intention for the lesson. Learning intentions describe what students are expected to learn, whereas learning experiences describe the tasks that are designed to ensure that students learn. There's nothing wrong with sharing an agenda or describing tasks, but the learning intention focuses more critically on what students will learn from those activities.

STEPS IN DEVELOPING A LEARNING INTENTION

1 **Analyze the standards and identify concepts.** The concepts are generally found in the nouns and noun phrases. The concepts are the content, or the what, that students must learn.

2 **Identify the skills.** The skills are generally found in the verbs and verb phrases. The skills describe how students will demonstrate their understanding and point to the standard's rigor level. These skills are communicated through the success criteria, which we will address in a moment.

3 **Sequence the concepts and skills in a logical flow.** Teachers and teams identify which concepts and skills come first and which should come later. This helps identify the instructional materials that will be useful for learning.

4 **Identify student-facing statements that inform students about what they are learning.** Based on the standards and what students need to learn, teachers develop and share statements that are explicit. Students do not have to infer what they are expected to learn.

NOUNS
WHAT

VERBS
(HOW)

COMMON VERBS (SKILLS) THAT STUDENTS NEED TO LEARN:

Analyze Apply Cite Classify Compare Compose Comprehend Demonstrate Describe Determine Develop Differentiate Distinguish Draw Evaluate Explain Express Generate Identify Infer Interpret Justify Organize Paraphrase Recognize Retell Specify State Summarize Support Synthesize Verify

THE CONCEPTS AND SKILLS STUDENTS NEED TO LEARN INCLUDE:

Concepts (nouns)	Skills (verbs)
• Theme • Story, drama, or poem • Details • Text	• Determine • Summarize

Determine a theme of a story, drama, or poem from details in the text; summarize the text. (English Language Arts Common Core State Standards, Grade 4)

Example Learning Intention:
Today, we are learning about the theme of a story, so that we can summarize what we read.

BEST PRACTICES FOR QUALITY LEARNING INTENTIONS[12]

☐ Learning intentions are visible and usable for students.

☐ Learning intentions are discussed at the lesson's beginning, middle, and end.

☐ Students are given time to reflect, ask questions, and discuss learning intentions.

☐ Connections are made to the learning intentions while students are engaged in the learning.

☐ Students are asked to monitor their progress using the learning intentions.

☐ Learning intentions are directly connected to the standard(s).

WHY AM I LEARNING THIS?

The second question focuses on relevance. Students who find their learning relevant are more likely to engage in learning tasks and regulate their behavior. When content is relevant, students devote their time, effort, and energy to learning.

Students expect to have

COMPETENCE
believing that you have the ability to be successful in accomplishing goals, also called efficacy

AUTONOMY
having some control over what you do, when you do it, and whom you do it with

RELATEDNESS
feeling connected to others and cared about by people you respect

Notice in our example learning intention on page 27, we shared the "why." Why do we need to learn about the theme of a story? So that we can summarize what we read.

ADDRESSING RELEVANCE ON A CONTINUUM

Relevance occurs across a continuum, and all of these can be used to invite students into learning.[13]

PERSONAL ASSOCIATION ➞ **PERSONAL USEFULNESS** ➞ **PERSONAL IDENTIFICATION**

Personal association is through a connection to an object or memory, such as enjoying reading about horses because the student is learning to ride one. When students make connections to their personal experiences, it can spark interest.

Personal usefulness is based on students' beliefs that a task or text will help them reach a personal goal. For example, a student reads articles about soccer because improving passing skills is valued. Or students persevere through a mathematics course because they believe that the knowledge will help them gain admission to a specific college.

Personal identification is the most motivating type of relevancy and stems from a deep understanding that the task or text aligns with one's identity. When students get to learn about themselves, their problem-solving, and their ability to impact others, relevance is increased. For example, a student who reads about female scientists sees herself in their experiences, further shaping her aspirations.

Source: Making Learning Personally Meaningful: A New Framework for Relevance Research, Helen Dwight Reid Educational Foundation, The Journal of experimental education, reprinted by permission of Informa UK Limited, trading as Taylor & Francis Group, www.tandfonline.com

BEST PRACTICES FOR MAKING LEARNING RELEVANT[14]

☐ There is a consideration of the lesson's relevancy connection before instruction.

☐ Relevancy statements are closely connected to students and not to a distant goal.

☐ Providing the relevancy statement supports students moving from declarative to procedural and conditional knowledge.

☐ Relevancy statements allow students to make a personal association (a connection to an object or memory).

☐ Relevancy statements promote the belief that a task or text will help students reach a personal goal.

☐ Relevancy is provided so students recognize that the task or text aligns with their identities and ability to impact others.

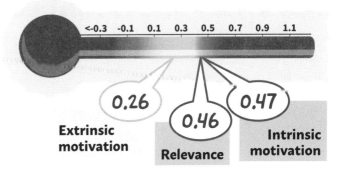

Extrinsic motivation 0.26
Relevance 0.46
Intrinsic motivation 0.47

Relevance is part of **motivation**, which has an average effect size of **0.39**. Motivation in the classroom can be divided into two categories: intrinsic and extrinsic. **Intrinsic motivation** has an effect size of **0.47**, whereas **extrinsic motivation** has an effect size of **0.26.**

Teachers use both types of motivation to push students along in their learning, but building intrinsic motivation helps students feel satisfied and accomplished, and learn more.

A more comprehensive model of motivation and engagement has four dimensions:[15]

Task: perceptions of the value of the task, its usefulness, and its importance

Goals: the acceptance of a goal and the belief that the goal is worth the effort

Self: expectations of success, self-efficacy, and confidence

Costs and benefits: an assessment of the amount of effort required to obtain the benefit, which may be a grade, avoidance of a negative consequence, or satisfaction in a job well done

Motivation is not about getting students to do something, but rather encouraging them to do it and not something else. It's always a trade-off, and we choose to do one thing over other things that we could do. The four dimensions predict which way the decision will go; and answering the second clarity question—***why am I learning this?***—helps address several of the factors related to motivation.

HOW WILL I KNOW THAT I LEARNED IT?

This final clarity question focuses on what it means to have learned something. Learning is invisible as it happens in our heads, and a major aim is to make the processes and strategies of learning more visible to students and teachers.

Success criteria help make the learning visible. Students should know what successful learning looks like. After all, experiencing success is another motivator, and we all enjoy the flood of joy and satisfaction that comes with success. Success criteria are designed to signal to learners about the destination and provide a map for how they will get there.

Typically, success criteria start with *"I can ..."* but can also be shared via rubrics, checklists, teacher modeling, or student work samples and exemplars. Regardless of the format, success criteria focus on something students will say, do, make, or write to indicate they are making progress toward the learning intention.

I can monitor my emotional response when learning gets hard.

I can determine the absolute value of a real number.

I can ask questions when I am confused.

I can retell a story from beginning to middle to end.

Co-constructing success criteria with students allows them to more deeply understand what successful learning looks like, and then to use the tools to monitor their progress and assess their own learning. Students who have input on determining what comprises successful completion get to explore the purpose, not just the logistics, of the task in advance. In addition, co-constructing success criteria increases students' confidence that they will meet the expectations because they have had a hand in determining what those are.

Teachers can start with projects and assignments with concrete visual examples or rubrics to help students understand how to co-construct success criteria. Many teachers save exemplars of their favorite projects; if so, this might be a good starting point to introduce a task and extend the invitation to develop success criteria jointly with your class.

BEST PRACTICES FOR QUALITY SUCCESS CRITERIA[16]

☐ Success criteria are visible and usable for students.

☐ Success criteria are shared and clarified with students before, during, and after learning.

☐ Success criteria communicate I will know I have learned it when I can... with specific parts or steps needed for success.

☐ Success criteria include work examples, exemplars, or models for clarity.

☐ Students are asked to use the success criteria to self-assess learning progress.

☐ Students are asked to provide feedback to peers using success criteria.

☐ Success criteria are used to provide feedback to students.

☐ Each criterion for success moves the students incrementally closer to the learning intention.

TIPS FOR CO-CONSTRUCTING SUCCESS CRITERIA

• Place learners into small groups. Give students examples of previous work, exemplars, to analyze, and ask them to identify the level of performance. Allow time for discourse and debate. Move among groups to ask clarifying and probing questions.

• Ask students to identify essential characteristics of each sample.

• Ask groups to share the criteria selected, determine commonalities across the class, and negotiate which criteria will be included in the final success criteria.

• Once success criteria have been determined, decide on the approach for showing and knowing expectations of success (e.g., *I can* statements, a single-point rubric, an analytic/holistic rubric).

VL Signature Practice #3:

PHASES OF LEARNING

PHASES OF LEARNING

Learning begins at the **surface level**. But that does not mean superficial. Rather, it consists of foundational and introductory concepts and skills that students must learn. Another way of thinking about surface learning is "***knowing that***"—the stuff that students must initially learn.

With intentional experiences, learning moves from surface to deep. **Deep learning** requires that students see the connections between and among the concepts and skills they are learning. Another way of thinking about deep learning is "***knowing how***"—how to use the knowledge.

And, with different experiences, learning can move to the **transfer level**, which is really the goal of our collective efforts. At the transfer level, students can use the concepts and skills on their own in a range of new experiences. At this phase, the focus is on "***knowing with***."

SURFACE LEARNING

Knowing That: Skill and concept development

DEEP LEARNING

Knowing How: Connections, relationships, and schema to organize skills and concepts

TRANSFER OF LEARNING

Knowing With: Self-regulation to continue learning skills and content, applying knowledge to new situations

Surface and deep learning consist of two subphases: **acquisition** and **consolidation**.

During **acquisition**, students are introduced to information and they process it in their working memory. This phase requires that students acquire, process, and understand information, often from a teacher but also from reading or other input experiences.[17]

Consolidation requires that the learner practice and rehearse the information, which increases the likelihood that the information moves into long-term memory. Consolidation allows students to integrate new information with what they already know, connect concepts with each other, and create a mental model that allows for use of the information.

Thus, the **VISIBLE LEARNING** model of learning looks more like this:[18]

SURFACE

"Knowing that" acquiring

"Knowing that" consolidating

DEEP

"Knowing how" acquiring

"Knowing how" consolidating

"Knowing with" transfer

TRANSFER

And there are specific strategies that are effective at each phase of learning. Deep learning strategies don't work any better for surface learning than surface learning strategies work for deep learning.

VL SIGNATURE PRACTICE #3: PHASES OF LEARNING   **35**

ACQUIRING SURFACE LEARNING

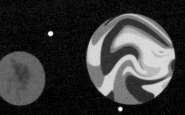

Integrating prior knowledge (ES = 0.96). Intentionally making connections with content students already know.

Mnemonics (ES = 0.65). Creating memory aids by using the initial letters of a statement to help students remember, such as this saying to remember the planets in our solar system:

My Very Excellent Mother Just Served Us Nachos

Vocabulary instruction (ES = 0.62). Teaching students word meanings and how to figure out unknown words from word parts (morphology) and context clues.

Outlining and summarizing (ES = 0.62). Recording main ideas and details in a written form or summarizing information recently learned.

Direct instruction (ES = 0.56). Providing explicit information, often in small increments, to develop a specific skill.

CONSOLIDATING SURFACE LEARNING

Rehearsal and memorization (ES = 0.71). Tasks that allow for repeated practice and multiple exposures to over-learn and memorize.

Help-seeking (ES = 0.73). Knowing when to ask for help and on what specific aspect of the learning help is required.

Strategy instruction (ES = 0.60). Teaching problem-solving techniques and strategies such as visualizing, predicting, comparing, clarifying as part of the learning process.

Spaced versus mass practice (ES = 0.59). Practicing over time and not all at once; not trying to cram information into your brain.

Rereading (ES = 0.50). Structuring tasks such that students read the text multiple times, typically for different tasks or questions.

Underlining and highlighting (ES = 0. 42). Marking a text while reading, identifying key ideas and important details.

Wide reading / exposure to reading (ES = 0.50). Reading regularly, which builds background knowledge and vocabulary.

Working memory training (ES = 0.37). Completing tasks that allow for practice in recalling items from working memory.

Note-taking (ES = 0.33). Recording information presented by another person or while reading and organizing it in written form.

Practice testing (ES = 0.49). Taking a practice version of an assessment, scoring it, and deciding what you still need to study or learn.

Interleaved practice (ES = 0.46). Learning two or more concepts and practicing them in alternating ways Focus on one topic, move to a different topic, return to first, etc.

Test-taking strategies (ES = 0.24). Teaching students how tests work, the format of questions, and how to demonstrate knowledge and skills on a specific test.

ACQUIRING DEEP LEARNING

Elaboration and organization (ES = 0.75). Building on what students already know to expand their understanding of how knowledge is organized.

Elaborative interrogation (ES = 0.59). Students generating an explanation for why a fact or concept is true. Students ask themselves a question such as "why does this make sense?" and work through their answer to the question.

Strategy monitoring (ES = 0.54). Students monitoring the problem-solving techniques and strategies they use while learning. Students are taught techniques and strategies during surface learning and then monitor their use during deep learning.

Self-judgment and reflection (ES = 0.81). Students learning to reflect on their own work and make an informed judgment about the quality of the work and how it compares with the expectations.

Meta-cognitive strategies (ES = 0.52). Techniques to help students understand their thinking processes as they learn and allow them to plan, monitor, and assess their own learning.

CONSOLIDATING DEEP LEARNING

Organizing and transforming notes (ES = .85). Using the notes that have been taken and creating something new from them, such as a visual representation, key points, or outlines.

Reciprocal Teaching (ES = 0.74). Pausing while reading to have a conversation with peers in which the comprehension strategies of predicting, clarifying, questioning, and summarizing are practiced.

Study skills (ES = 0.50). Students making choices about cognitive, metacognitive, and effective ways to study, such as setting goals, managing time, monitoring progress, summarizing information, or creating flashcards.

Classroom discussion (ES = 0.82). Inviting students to interact with their peers with extended exchanges of information, allowing them to agree and disagree, using academic language.

Concept mapping (ES = 0.62). Creating graphic organizers and other visual displays that require identifying relationships between ideas.

Self-verbalization and self-questioning (ES = 0.58). Talking to oneself about and through difficult academic tasks as well as asking increasingly complex questions of oneself while reading or engaged in a task.

Collaborative learning (ES = 0.45). Grouping students in small groups and ensuring that each student has a role or task to contribute to the group.

TRANSFER LEARNING

Jigsaw (ES = 1.20). Useful at the surface and deep levels as well, jigsaw provides an opportunity for transfer when students identify similarities and differences between the sections of the text following their expert and home-group conversations.

Synthesizing information across texts (ES =0.63). Reading several pieces of text and then verbally or in writing, synthesizing information, noting similarities and differences across the documents, recognizing different points of view or perspectives, and drawing conclusions or making a critical evaluation.

Formal discussions (ES = 0.82). Structuring class discussion in ways that require students to use knowledge and skills in new or novel ways. Socratic seminars and debates are examples of formal discussions.

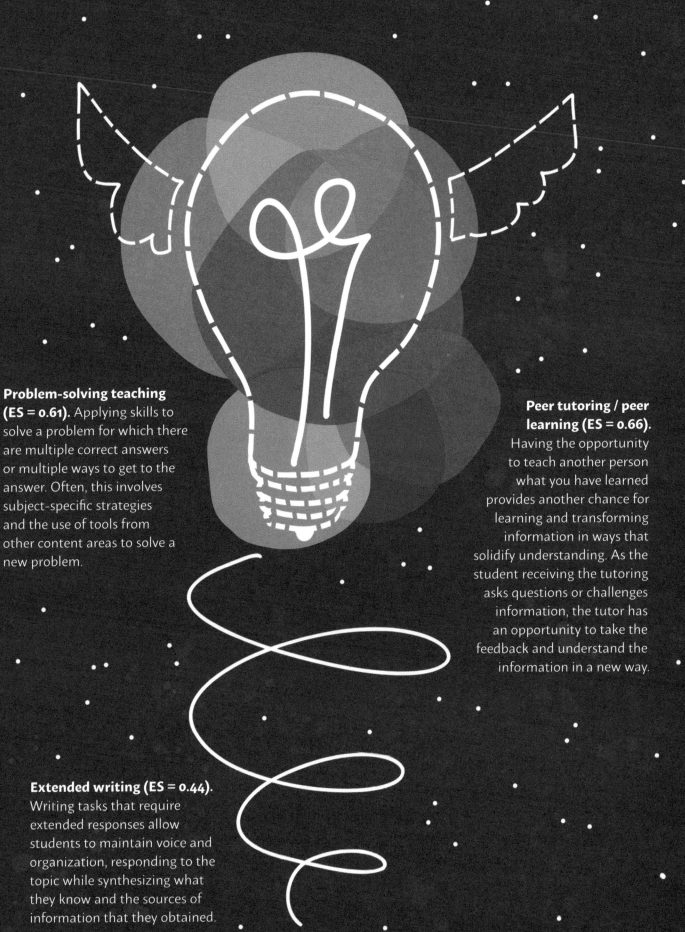

Problem-solving teaching (ES = 0.61). Applying skills to solve a problem for which there are multiple correct answers or multiple ways to get to the answer. Often, this involves subject-specific strategies and the use of tools from other content areas to solve a new problem.

Peer tutoring / peer learning (ES = 0.66). Having the opportunity to teach another person what you have learned provides another chance for learning and transforming information in ways that solidify understanding. As the student receiving the tutoring asks questions or challenges information, the tutor has an opportunity to take the feedback and understand the information in a new way.

Extended writing (ES = 0.44). Writing tasks that require extended responses allow students to maintain voice and organization, responding to the topic while synthesizing what they know and the sources of information that they obtained.

VL Signature Practice #4:

TEACHING STUDENTS TO DRIVE THEIR LEARNING

TEACHING STUDENTS TO DRIVE THEIR LEARNING

Engagement is an important aspect of learning. Students who find their learning relevant are more likely to engage. Students who are motivated are more likely to engage. In fact, engagement occurs across a continuum, from disrupting to driving.[19]

ACTIVE DISENGAGEMENT PASSIVE

Disrupting	Avoiding	Withdrawing
Distracting others	Looking for ways to avoid work	Being distracted
Disrupting the learning environment	Off-task behaviors	Physically separating from group
Engaging in problematic behavior	Packing backpack before class ends	Daydreaming
Destruction of materials	Using various excuses to leave the classroom	Sleeping in class
Persistent talking about something other than the topic of the lesson	Returning to class late from a break	Acting or imitating participation
Speaking with unkind words		Hyper-focusing on a task other than the one at hand

We have identified six characteristics of students who drive their learning.[20] We also think of these as visible learners and assessment-capable learners.

Know their current level of understanding

Know where they're going and are confident they can take on the challenge

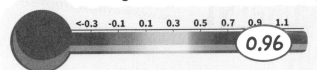

Teaching students to drive their learning

<-0.3 -0.1 0.1 0.3 0.5 0.7 0.9 1.1

0.96

It's the *Driving* column, below right, that is the focus of this signature practice. Teaching students to drive their learning ensures that students are self-regulated.

PASSIVE **ENGAGEMENT** ACTIVE

Participating	Investing	Driving
Doing work	Asking questions	Setting goals for themselves based on what the class is learning
Paying attention	Valuing the learning	Seeking feedback from others
Responding to questions	Recognizing that there are things worth learning	Self-assessing and monitoring progress
Observe teachers doing work	Collaborating with peers	Teaching others
Following teacher instructions	Talking about their learning with others	Being inspired to learn more about a topic or pursue an interest
Complying with a new rule	Thinking along with their teachers	

FEEDBACK AHEAD

Select tools to guide their learning

Seek feedback and recognize that errors are opportunities to learn

Monitor their progress and adjust their learning

Recognize their learning and can teach others

LEARNERS KNOW THEIR CURRENT LEVEL OF UNDERSTANDING

It's hard to know where you are going if you don't know where you are. Students should be informed of their current levels of understanding or performance. It should not be a secret, nor should it be a source of shame or embarrassment.

Conferencing. Spending time with students and talking about their current performance levels is time well spent. To manage the numbers, teachers can meet with 10% of their students daily, allowing them to meet with all students over two weeks. These short conversations focus on strengths and current levels of understanding.

Initial assessments. Teachers can check with students about what they already know at the start of a unit or lesson. These brief assessments help students understand where they are in the learning journey and can motivate them as they understand that there is learning to be done.

Self-assessment. Teachers can develop tools that allow students to determine their current level of performance. Checklists and rubrics are samples of tools that students can use to assess their current level of performance. You can also turn your "*I can*" success criteria statements into "*Can I*" statements that invite students to consider what they can already do.

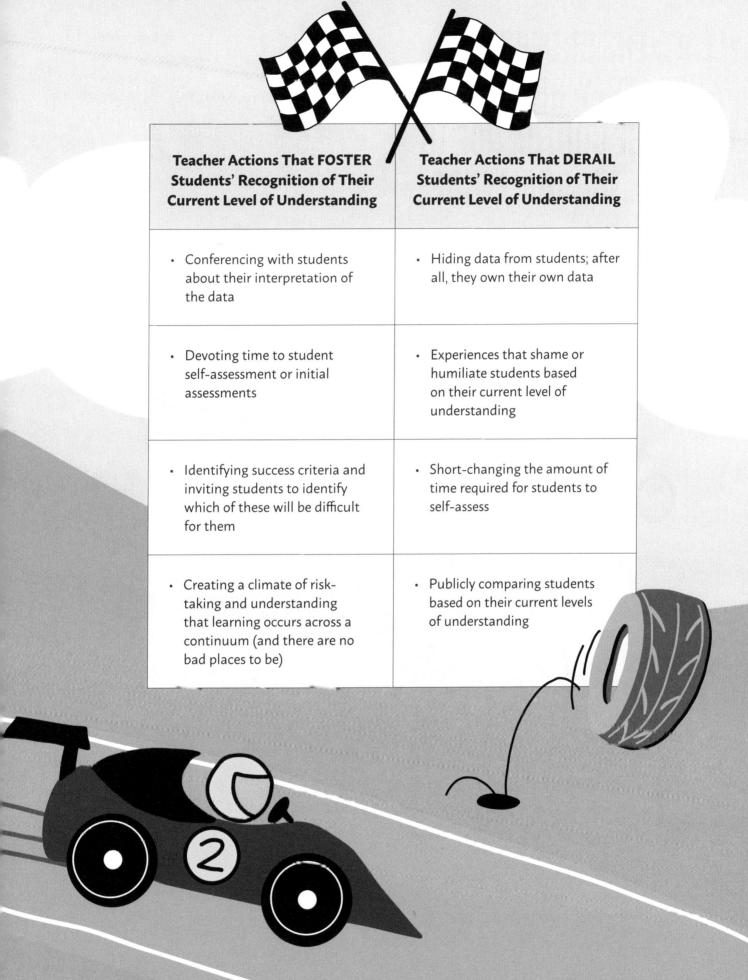

Teacher Actions That FOSTER Students' Recognition of Their Current Level of Understanding	Teacher Actions That DERAIL Students' Recognition of Their Current Level of Understanding
• Conferencing with students about their interpretation of the data	• Hiding data from students; after all, they own their own data
• Devoting time to student self-assessment or initial assessments	• Experiences that shame or humiliate students based on their current level of understanding
• Identifying success criteria and inviting students to identify which of these will be difficult for them	• Short-changing the amount of time required for students to self-assess
• Creating a climate of risk-taking and understanding that learning occurs across a continuum (and there are no bad places to be)	• Publicly comparing students based on their current levels of understanding

LEARNERS UNDERSTAND WHERE THEY'RE GOING AND HAVE THE CONFIDENCE TO TAKE ON THE CHALLENGE

When students have access to learning intentions and success criteria, they have a sense of where they are going. When they also know their current level of performance, they can compare that with the destination. With these two aspects in place—current levels of understanding and a destination—students are much more likely to take on the challenge of learning.

Students often speak of tasks (assignments) on a single continuum: **easy to difficult**.

But this is only half the story when it comes to challenging tasks. There's another continuum, which is **complexity**. **Some tasks are more complex, while others are less so.**

These two terms seem to be used interchangeably, but in fact they are two different constructs. **Difficulty** is a measure of the amount of effort, time, or work needed, while **complexity** is a measure of the number of cognitive steps or potential outcomes. The tasks we design for our students should be a balance of difficulty and complexity. We need our students to:

EXERCISE STRATEGIC THINKING
(low difficulty/high complexity), such as tasks requiring metacognition, goal setting, or new learning tools

ENCOUNTER SITUATIONS WHERE THEY STRUGGLE
(high difficulty/high complexity), such as project-based learning or close readings

INCREASE THEIR FLUENCY
(low difficulty/low complexity), such as applying past knowledge, using a familiar graphic organizer, or taking notes

BUILD THEIR STAMINA
(high difficulty/low complexity), such as independent reading or writing research papers

Teacher Actions That FOSTER Students' Knowledge About Where They Are Going and Encourage Them to Accept the Challenge of Learning	Teacher Actions That DERAIL Students' Knowledge About Where They Are Going and Discourage Them From Accepting the Challenge of Learning
• Planning out instruction, including accurate explanations, examples, and guided practice	• Asking students to set goals without the teacher having a clear understanding of the goal
• Allocating time during instruction for students to understand the path of learning, and self-assess their current progression	• Expecting students to monitor their progress without providing a model for how to self-assess
• Providing choice in how students demonstrate mastery of the success criteria	• Expecting students to monitor progress and set goals without providing time and opportunities to monitor success against the success criteria
• Using student interests to develop learning experiences that resonate with them	• Not recognizing that each year the students have different interests and unique identities
• Promoting academic self-efficacy by creating high-trust and excellent relations among students so that it is ok to make and learn from mistakes	

LEARNERS SELECT TOOLS TO GUIDE THEIR LEARNING

Knowing where you are, knowing where you need to be, and recognizing the challenge are important aspects of learning. Accomplishing the required learning requires tools. In the learning module, we focused on tools useful at the surface, deep, and transfer phases. What we did not say was that students needed to be taught these tools and then be allowed to make choices about which tools to use and when.

There is not an endless list of tools for a given learning task. In fact, too many tools can be overwhelming for students, and they might think their teachers don't know how to teach. But there is often more than one useful tool. Importantly, students will make mistakes and choose tools that do not work. That's part of the learning process: recognizing when a tool does not work and then deciding what to do when you're not sure what to do.

Graphic organizers and concept maps

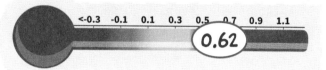

Graphic organizers and concept maps, with an effect size of **0.62**, are good examples of teaching tools with several iterations that students can select from. Teachers can introduce a range of graphic organizers and then create situations in which students select one to complete. Graphic organizers are not an end product, but should be used to prepare for another task, such as a discussion or writing assignment.

COMMON GRAPHIC ORGANIZERS

VENN

Overlapping circles that illustrate similarities and differences between two concepts

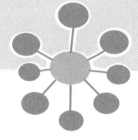

WEB

Central word or phrase linked to supporting labels, concepts, and ideas

SEQUENCE/PROCESS

To show a series of steps or a timeline

FRAYER MODEL[21]

Four-celled table for recording information about a term or concept; information recorded inside the cells could be examples and non-examples, definitions, synonyms and antonyms, the term used in context, an illustration or drawing, and more

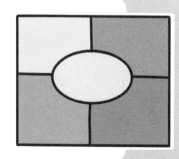

Teacher Actions That FOSTER Students' Ability to Select Tools to Guide Their Learning	Teacher Actions That DERAIL Students' Ability to Select Tools to Guide Their Learning
• Introducing students to a range of tools	• Asking students to choose a tool without introducing and modeling those tools first
• Providing opportunities for students to practice using tools	• Preselecting all tools for students
• Structuring learning tasks so students can make choices about which tools to use	• Providing little opportunity for students to use tools or strategies that have been introduced
• Asking students to reflect on the effectiveness of the strategy or tool that they chose	• Discouraging mistakes in the tool selection process
	• Skipping the time to reflect on the process, and on the tools and strategies students selected

STORY MAP

To show different elements such as characters, plots, themes, etc.

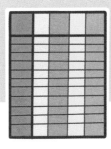

CHART/MATRIX

Rows and columns in a table format that shows relationships vertically and horizontally

T-CHART

Two-column table for grouping ideas into categories

PROBLEM-SOLUTION MAP

Identifies a problem and possible solutions, often with pros and cons for each solution

LEARNERS MONITOR THEIR PROGRESS AND ADJUST THEIR LEARNING

With appropriate tools, students can monitor their progress and note when they are on track and need to make adjustments or take action to improve their learning. Without such tools, students are dependent on the teacher to inform them that they are, or are not, progressing in their learning journey. Dependency on the teacher harms learning.

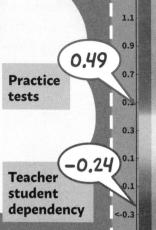

Practice tests 0.49

Teacher student dependency −0.24

CAN I?

I CAN!

Practice tests are another way that students can monitor their own learning.

Practice tests provide students an opportunity to take short quizzes to understand their progress in the subject or topic. These formative opportunities are low stake and not part of the student's grade, as the emphasis here is on practice to gain self-knowledge of learning gaps. Importantly:

The success criteria "**I can**" statements, rubrics, and checklists can all be used to teach students to monitor their progress. It's this continued self-assessment that allows students to drive their own learning.

- Feedback paired with the practice test enhances learning.
- The usefulness of practice tests was strong at both the elementary and secondary levels.[22]
- The value of practice tests is in students' reflecting on their results.

One way to teach students to adjust their learning with a practice test is to teach them a range of learning strategies and then invite them to make choices about which to use based on where they are in the learning cycle.

Cognitive Study Skills	Metacognitive Study Skills	Affective Study Skills
• Note-taking • Graphic organizers (creating and using) • Summarizing • Practice and rehearsal techniques (e.g., flashcards, mnemonics, memorization) • Rereading	• Planning for the task • Monitoring one's learning • Reviewing and revising corrected work • Self-assessment • Self-questioning	• Motivation to study • Building confidence to take on challenges • Belief in its usefulness • Agency to influence one's learning • Willingness to solve problems • Managing stress and anxiety • Goal setting

Teacher Actions That FOSTER Students' Ability to Monitor Their Progress and Adjust Their Learning	Teacher Actions That DERAIL Students' Ability to Monitor Their Progress and Adjust Their Learning
• Intentionally build moments into a lesson that allow for students to reflect on their progress	• Expecting students to just know how to write goals for themselves
• Changing "I can" statements into "Can I?" so students can reflect on what they have learned and set their next goal	• Evaluating student learning without helping students monitor their own progress
• Explicitly teach and model planning and organizing strategies	• Asking students to engage in problem-based learning before they have the foundational skills and knowledge needed to apply their learning
• Structuring tasks so that students are required to interact with one another	• Shying away from challenging students with complex tasks

LEARNERS SEEK FEEDBACK AND RECOGNIZE THAT ERRORS ARE OPPORTUNITIES TO LEARN

Notice that this says **seek** feedback, rather than **receive** feedback. Students who drive their own learning actively seek help and feedback from their peers and teachers. Teachers, and peers, may provide significant amounts of feedback that doesn't change a thing. When we seek feedback, we are all much more likely to accept and act upon that feedback. The key to great feedback is: *Was the feedback heard, understood, and actioned?*

The four dimensions of student feedback literacy, meaning their understanding of the role of feedback, include:[23]

1. Appreciating feedback as a means to strengthen their learning, while also understanding that feedback comes in a variety of forms and sources. In addition, knowing that acting on the feedback will enhance their efforts.

2. Making judgments so they can accurately judge their own work and the work of peers, and participate in peer critique opportunities

3. Managing affect to avoid being defensive, and making it a habit to seek feedback from others

4. Taking action is a product of the first three, in that students must act upon the feedback and have a repertoire of strategies for doing so

Seeking feedback requires that students understand that errors are opportunities to learn and not the source of embarrassment, shame, or humiliation. This comes from the climate of the classroom that has been created and maintained by the teacher and the students. Feedback frames can help normalize the process of seeking and receiving feedback.

Giving	Receiving
• I noticed that . . .	• I appreciate you noticing that . . .
• I wondered about . . .	• I hadn't thought about that . . .
• I was confused by . . .	• I heard you say that _____ confused you.
• I suggest that . . .	• Based on your suggestion, I will . . .
• Have you thought about . . .	• Thank you, what would you do?
• You might consider . . .	• I'm not sure what that looks like, tell me more.

Students should understand that there are four possible learning events:

*Of the four conditions, **unproductive failure** yields the smallest gains, as students' thinking is not guided in any way, and they are just expected to discover what should be learned.*

***Unproductive success** is also of limited value, as students in this condition primarily rely on memorization but don't ever get to why and how this is applied. There's just no transfer of knowledge.*

UNPRODUCTIVE FAILURE
(unguided problem solving)

UNPRODUCTIVE SUCCESS
(memorizing an algorithm, without understanding why)

PRODUCTIVE FAILURE
(using prior knowledge to figure out a solution, followed by more instruction)

PRODUCTIVE SUCCESS
(structured problem solving)

*But for students to drive their own learning, they need to also experience **productive failure**. Learning from errors ensures learners persist in generating and exploring representations and solutions, incorporating the support they receive from others.*

*In **productive success** conditions, students are guided to resolve problems (not just memorize formulas).*

Teacher Actions That FOSTER Students' Ability to Seek Feedback and Recognize That Errors Are Opportunities to Learn	Teacher Actions That DERAIL Students' Ability to Seek Feedback and Recognize That Errors Are Opportunities to Learn
• Modeling seeking feedback and the excitement of using feedback to make improvements	• Assuming that the feedback given was received.
• Modeling making mistakes and how you learned something from the mistake	• Waiting until the end of the assignment to provide feedback
• Leveraging clear success criteria to support peer-to-peer feedback	• Asking students to give peer-to peer feedback without clear communication of the success criteria
• Giving students the opportunity to use what they know before stepping in to refine knowledge or further develop skills	• Asking students to memorize information or complete tasks without understanding the relevance

LEARNERS RECOGNIZE THEIR LEARNING AND TEACH OTHERS

The tools students use to monitor their progress also help them recognize their success in learning and where they need to next move to enhance their learning. Students learn that there are different kinds of learning. "Whether you need to learn a new skill (action-based), grow awareness or change attitudes (emotion-based), or acquire new cognitive concepts (knowledge-based),"[24] students can learn to ask themselves:

1. *What new habits do I have to build during the learning process?*
2. *What level of knowledge do I need to demonstrate?*

WHEN LEARNING HAS OCCURRED, WE CAN:

- demonstrate it any time and any place,
- do things that used to be difficult with more ease,
- perform new skills or recall information,
- recognize that our behavior, thinking, or feelings have changed, and
- most critically, when we have learned, *we can teach others.*

When students have the opportunity to recognize their learning and teach others, they are actually relearning concepts and skills. The effects on the student-teacher are higher than on the students being taught—although all have high positive effects. As some have argued, when you teach content, you get to learn it again. There are a lot of peer tutoring models that provide students with opportunities to recognize their learning and teach others.[25]

Classwide Peer Tutoring (CWPT): At specific times each week, the class is divided into groups of two to five students. The goal is to practice or review skills and content, rather than introduce new learning. Each student in the group has an opportunity to be both the tutee and tutor. The teacher typically assigns the content to be covered during these sessions, which includes a peer explaining the work, asking questions of the group, and providing the feedback to the peer(s).

Cross-Age Peer Tutoring: Older students are paired with younger students, and the older students have the responsibility to serve as the tutor. The older student is the tutor even though current peformance levels may be similar. The tutors explain concepts, model appropriate behavior, ask questions, and encourage better study habits. Tutors may even be taught to design lessons for their younger students.

Peer Assisted Learning Strategies (PALS): Pairs of students work together, taking turns tutoring and being tutored. Teachers train students to use the following learning strategies for reading: passage reading with partners, paragraph "shrinking" (or describing the main idea), and prediction relay (predicting what is likely to happen next in the passage).

Teacher Actions That INCREASE Students' Understanding of What They Learned and Their Ability to Teach Others	Teacher Actions That DERAIL Students' Understanding of What They Learned and Their Ability to Teach Others
• Providing instruction on how to give growth-producing feedback	• Expecting students to use a rubric to self-assess with criterion that hasn't been modeled or processed
• Planning opportunities for students to interpret the data and information gained from examining formative practice assessments	• Providing opportunities for peers to give each other feedback without training students in how to give feedback
• Placing value on the act of examining one's own work over the correctness of that work	• Setting up peer-tutoring experiences without students having solidified their own skills
• Allowing students to hear the internal decision-making process of teachers	• Setting up peer-tutoring experiences with some students never getting the opportunity to be the tutor
• Fostering a culture of supportive peer relationships	
• Making intentional decisions about how to partner students	

Same-Age Peer Tutoring: As with class wide peer tutoring, there are opportunities to create tutoring structures across a grade level or content area. In some cases, the same-age peers are within the same classroom, and other times they collaborate across classrooms. In same-age tutoring, not all the students are engaged in tutoring at the same time, as would be the case for CWPT. Again, the teacher trains the tutors on their role and establishes routines for the same-age tutoring.

Reciprocal Peer Tutoring (RPT): In this format of peer tutoring, students are paired at random to support the learning of their peers. It's a collaborative learning task involving students with similar academic backgrounds working together. Each partnership is responsible for synthesizing content, preparing tasks, and asking questions complete with answers and explanation. Often students develop practice tests during RPT and then identify areas of additional learning needed.

Teach Back: Providing students opportunities to teach back what they have learned is good for their learning, and it's a great opportunity for determining what has stuck and if there are any misconceptions. And this is not limited to in-class interactions. Students can teach their siblings, parents, or extended family members. They can teach back to the class or directly to the teacher.

THE ILLUSTRATED GUIDE TO VISIBLE LEARNING

VL Signature Practice #5:

TEACHING WITH INTENT

TEACHING WITH INTENT

There is no one right way to teach. And no instructional strategies are guaranteed to ensure learning for all students. In fact, we believe that educators should not hold any teaching strategy in higher esteem than students' learning.

The instructional experiences and strategies must impact learning, or they must be changed.

It's one of the key ideas and is represented in several mindframes.

Intentional, systematic, and targeted teaching suggests that tools, techniques, and instructional strategies fit into four major categories, including[26]

TEACHER RESPONSIBILITY

FOCUSED INSTRUCTION

providing students with information about what they will learn as well as input that they can use during the learning process

GUIDED INSTRUCTION

scaffolding experiences without telling students what to think, which includes responding to errors and misconceptions

Educators should talk more about learning and less about teaching.

However, we recognize that there are strategies and routines that are more likely to ensure that learning occurs. And there are strategies and routines that have very little likelihood of having any impact. And there is a right and wrong time to use specific teaching strategies.

Source: Used with permission of ACSD from Better Learning Through Structured Teaching : A Framework for the Gradual Release of Responsibility, Fisher, D., Frey, N., 2021; permission conveyed through Copyright Clearance Center, Inc.

These four are based on a gradual release of responsibility framework that acknowledges that some parts of the lesson require that teachers work harder than the students and other parts of the lesson involve students working harder than the teacher. But highly accomplished teachers are not just gradual; they work on accelerating students' responsibility for learning. Perhaps this should be called **Accelerating Students' Responsibility for Learning**.

COLLABORATIVE LEARNING
engaging students in peer-to-peer learning using academic language and argumentation skills

INDEPENDENT LEARNING
assigning students tasks that allow for practice and application

Importantly, there is no prescribed order to these phases of learning, but each of them is important to close the loop for students.

Teachers can cycle through these phases several times in one lesson, returning to different phases throughout the experience.

COLLABORATIVE LEARNING

Students teaching and learning with their peers are much more likely to consolidate their understanding. In addition, they can practice and develop their academic language when they interact with others. **On average, the goal is to devote 50% of the instructional minutes each week to students interacting with and learning from peers.**

This requires classroom routines and structures that ensure that student-to-student interaction is effective and efficient. And it requires a meaningful task or question for groups to explore. Often students need to be taught how to work and learn with their peers. Having several go-to strategies helps students build their habits of interacting with you and each other.

Sometimes, **collaborative learning** occurs between you and the students.

This is known as **teacher-mediated discussion** because you interject often between students speaking, and there is much turn taking. Other times, it's **peer-mediated discussion** and collaboration, which will also free to you meet with small groups of students who need additional learning.

Collaborative learning allows students to engage with peers in a process of discovery. But we are not suggesting that teachers simply turn their classrooms over to students and have students control their own learning. Instead, during collaborative learning, students explore ideas, propositions, explanations, and solutions and take subsequent actions.

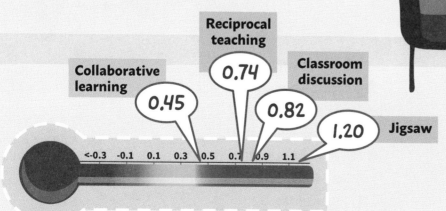

Collaborative learning 0.45

Reciprocal teaching 0.74

Classroom discussion 0.82

Jigsaw 1.20

<-0.3 -0.1 0.1 0.3 0.5 0.7 0.9 1.1

Note that students need sufficient surface learning to engage in most collaborative learning tasks.

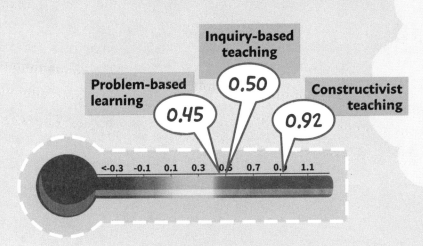

Problem-based learning **0.45**

Inquiry-based teaching **0.50**

Constructivist teaching **0.92**

LOOK-FORS IN COLLABORATIVE LEARNING

Discussion	• Students have opportunities to engage in discussions with peers. • The discussion is aligned with the academic learning and vocabulary of the lesson.
Routines	• The collaboration routine is familiar to students. If the routine is newer to students, it is accompanied with explicit instruction and modeling of the routine. • The collaboration routine used is developmentally appropriate.
Monitoring	• Student thinking is observed and monitored by the teacher. • The teacher provides affirmations and redirection when needed. • The teacher and students provide feedback to one another about the collaboration.
Task Design	• The task or problem is designed to promote intellectual interdependence. • The task is designed so that students use interpersonal skills and communication to successfully collaborate.
Links to Learning	• Students set goals before a collaborative task and monitor their success after the task. • Students are asked to draw conclusions and make connections to new or prior knowledge.

FOCUSED INSTRUCTION

This is the input phase of learning in which students gain new knowledge, skills, strategies, and concepts. It's often focused on surface-level learning, but teachers can also model complex thinking processes and ideas. This phase of learning is typically brief, under 15 minutes (less for younger students), but can occur many times during a lesson.

Some options teachers have to provide input include:

DIRECT INSTRUCTION
providing information directly and systematically for students

0.56

INTERACTIVE VIDEO
combining visual and language to share information

0.54

SIMULATIONS AND EXPERIMENTS
discovering information based on the experience designed for students

0.53

0.47

WORKED EXAMPLES
thinking aloud about a problem that has already been solved and explaining what the teacher sees in the example

1.1
0.9
0.7
0.5
0.3
0.1
-0.1
<-0.3

0.42

DEMONSTRATIONS
showing students something with an explanation provided

READING/READ ALOUDS
obtaining information from texts or having texts read aloud and discussed

MODELING
sharing examples and thinking aloud for students to approximate

LOOK-FORS IN FOCUSED INSTRUCTION

Pacing	• The time allotted for input and focus is developmentally appropriate. • The input and focus are concise and make efficient use of time. • The pace of the lesson is steady and consistent.
Rigor and Alignment	• The input and focus are grade-appropriate and aligned with standards or expectations for learning.
Statement of Goals	• The input and focus include a statement of the goal for the lesson. • The teacher names the skill, concept, or strategy being demonstrated.
Explanations and Examples	• Explanations are clear and developmentally appropriate. • Examples and non-examples illuminate the skill or concept being taught.
Modeling	• The input and focus include modeling the skill or concept and the decisions to use it.

GUIDED INSTRUCTION

When learners get stuck, teachers must know how to respond. This response, designed to improve understanding, correct an error, or address a misconception, leaves the student feeling either successful or helpless.

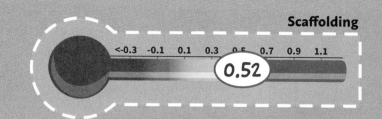

Scaffolding

<-0.3 -0.1 0.1 0.3 0.5 0.7 0.9 1.1

0.52

We call this phase of the teaching and learning process **guided instruction**. It represents a shared responsibility between the teacher and students. When guided instruction is done well, students feel supported, and teachers feel rewarded.

Guiding students' thinking can occur with the whole class, with smaller groups of students, or individually with students who need it. The process is the same, regardless of the number of students. The process requires scaffolding of students' thinking and not simply telling them what to think.

Guiding and **scaffolding** learning requires that the teacher use prompts and cues.

PROMPTS

CUES

PROMPTS	CUES
Background knowledge: Reference to content that the student already knows, has been taught, or has experienced but has temporarily forgotten or is not applying correctly	**Visual:** A range of graphic hints that guide students through thinking or understanding
Process or procedure: Reference to established or generally agreed-upon representation, rules, or guidelines that the student is not following due to error or misconception	**Verbal:** Variations in speech used to draw attention to something specific or verbal attention getters that focus students' thinking
Reflective: Promotion of metacognition—getting the student to think about his or her thinking—so that the student can use the resulting insight to determine next steps or the solution to a problem	**Gestural:** Teacher's body movements or motions used to draw attention to something that has been missed
Heuristic: Engagement in an informal, self-directed problem-solving procedure; the approach the student comes up with does not have to be like anyone else's approach, but it does need to work	**Environmental:** Using the surroundings, and things in the surroundings, to influence students' understanding

When prompts and cues don't work to resolve the issue, teachers need to resort to additional instruction, which might include modeling or direct explanation. Students cannot be left hanging. Teachers must ensure that students have a successful learning experience, even if that means giving the student the answer. Following the direct explanation, the teacher should monitor students' understanding by asking them to repeat the information in their own words or share their understanding with a peer.

LOOK-FORS IN GUIDED INSTRUCTION

Grouping	• The students are grouped according to similar instructional needs.
Goals	• The lesson goals are stated at the beginning and revisited at the end so that students can monitor their success.
Rigor	• The content of the lesson is complex and challenging for students. • The content of the lesson is grade-appropriate and aligned to standards or expectations.
Scaffolding	• The teacher used prompts and cues whenever possible to facilitate a cognitive lift on the part of learners. Students do the majority of explaining, making connections, and asking questions. • The teacher notices students' needs and is responsive, while fostering the independence of students whenever possible.

INDEPENDENT LEARNING TASKS

The goal of our lessons is to ensure that students develop skills that they can use on their own, and not just when the teacher is present. There are tasks that students can do in class on their own and tasks that can be assigned outside the classroom for students to complete.

There are some tasks that students can do at school, individually and independently, that provide them opportunities to practice and apply what they are learning.[27]

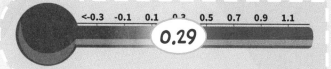

Homework

<-0.3   -0.1   0.1   0.3   0.5   0.7   0.9   1.1

0.29

YOU DO IT ALONE

- **Journal and essay writing.** Students can respond to prompts or tasks that require them to convey information, entertain readers, share an opinion, argue a perspective, or share an experience.

- **Independent reading.** Students can read from texts that have been assigned or texts that they have selected.

- **Designing, drafting, and completing projects.** Longer projects can be drafted at school, even if they are partially completed at home.

- **Performances and presentations.** Sharing with the class or wider audience allows students to practice organization and public speaking skills as well as to receive feedback from peers.

- **Preparing for discussions, debates, and Socratic seminars.** Students may need time at school to organize themselves and prepare for tasks that require that they interact with others.

- **Research.** Time to find things, including Internet searchers and visits to the library, are useful for students to investigate a topic as they prepare to use that information for another task, such as writing or debate or presentation.

There are also tasks that teachers can assign for students to complete outside of class.

The overall effect of homework is below average, but there is a difference in the effect when analyzed by grade bands. Homework is much more effective with **high school students (ES = 0.48)** than with **elementary students (ES = 0.15)**. That is mainly because high school typically allows them to practice skills that they have been taught. Elementary students too often get projects, and the impact of homework is likely to increase if this was changed to opportunities to deliberately practice what they have been taught at school.

We are not suggesting that independent learning be limited to class time. Instead, these out-of-class tasks should be short and should not require surveillance by adults at home. There are ways to develop effective homework assignments.[28]

Source: Fisher, Douglas, and Nancy Frey. "Homework and the Gradual Release of Responsibility: Making 'Responsibility' Possible." English Journal, vol. 98, no. 2, 2008, pp. 40-45. Copyright 2008 by the National Council of Teachers of English. Reprinted with permission.

Purpose of Homework	Characteristics	Reflective Questions
Fluency building	• Multiple opportunities for practice • Focuses on one or two skills • Serves as an access point for other skills or knowledge	1. Do students fully understand how the skill is performed? 2. Is the difficulty level appropriate so that they can focus on speed/rate/fluency, instead of how it is performed?
Application	• Allows a skill to be used to solve a problem, or apply a rule or principle • Uses previously learned skill for a new situation	1. What rule or principle will the students use to solve the problem? 2. Do the students possess the background knowledge and prior experiences necessary to understand the new or novel situation?
Spiral review	• Student utilizes previously learned skills or knowledge • Allows students to confirm their understanding and assess their own learning • Related conceptually to current learning	1. What previously taught skills or knowledge are important for future learning and assessment? 2. In what ways will this strengthen students' metacognitive awareness of how well they use skills and knowledge? 3. What previously taught skills or knowledge serve as a basis for current classroom instruction?
Extension	• Potential for development of new understandings • Results in a new product or innovation • Requires the use of a variety of skills or knowledge	1. Does the assignment lead to a new knowledge base or set of concepts? 2. Will the students create a new product or innovation that they have not done before? 3. What skills or knowledge will students require to complete the assignment?

LISTEN-FORS IN INDEPENDENT LEARNING

Teacher Knowledge and Decision-Making in Deliberate Practice	• Students have been taught about the role of deliberate practice (i.e., practice with feedback) in their learning. • The practice work is based on student learning data, including student feedback. • Practice work includes opportunities for students to set goals and self-assess.
Teacher Habits and Dispositions About Deliberate Practice	• Submitted practice work is accompanied by timely teacher feedback, usually within one week. • Student performance on practice work is used to inform future instruction. • A student who struggles to complete practice work is not labeled "unmotivated" but rather receives additional support to build practice habits.
Student Knowledge About Deliberate Practice	• Students know about the role of deliberate practice in their learning • Students view deliberate practice as being more than just a form of compliance. • Students know about the benefits of spaced and deliberate practice.
Student Habits and Dispositions About Deliberate Practice	• Students set deliberate practice goals for themselves. • Students engage in self-assessments that narrow their focus on what needs to be practiced.

VL Signature Practice #6:

PRACTICE AND OVER-LEARNING

VL SIGNATURE PRACTICE #6
PRACTICE AND OVER-LEARNING

The popular phrase *practice makes perfect* is not accurate. Practice can make something permanent, but only some types of practice ensure that learning occurs. But practice is, or can be, an important part of the learning process.

We have suggested that instruction should have an impact. In reality, we should probably say instruction and deliberate practice should have an impact. Deliberate practice is *practice with feedback*. The learning experiences that teachers design are only part of the equation. Students must practice, make mistakes, get feedback, try again, and so on to really learn. In that way, students move from acquiring concepts and skills to using them.

Students tend to acquire skills and concepts from instructional experiences. To move from acquisition to fluency, students must practice. To move from fluency to maintenance, more practice (and feedback) is required. Then to move from maintenance to generalization (or transfer), again more practice is required.[29]

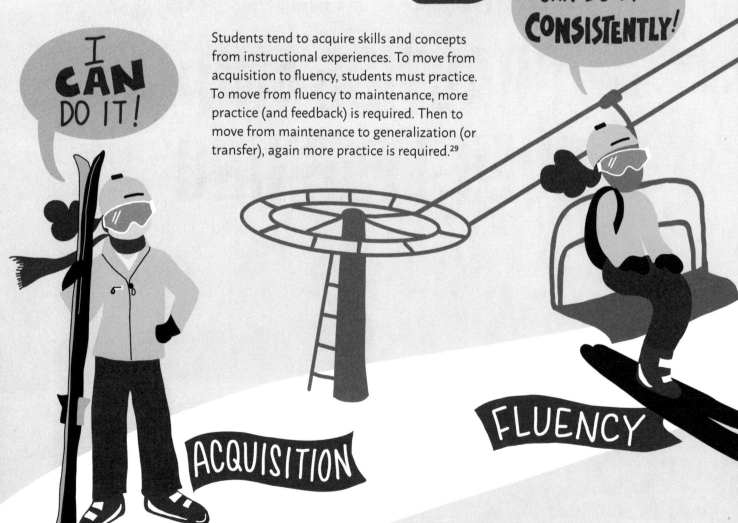

Repeated practice can allow students to over-learn.

Once something has been initially learned, additional deliberate practice can protect the memory from interference or decay. Over-learning can also help develop automaticity, the ability to do something without really thinking about it. However, engaging in repeated practice in one sitting probably does not ensure over-learning. Instead, as we noted in the section on homework, **spiral review** and **practicing** things over time are more likely to result in over-learning.

DELIBERATE PRACTICE

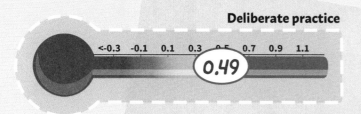

Deliberate practice

<-0.3 -0.1 0.1 0.3 0.5 0.7 0.9 1.1

0.49

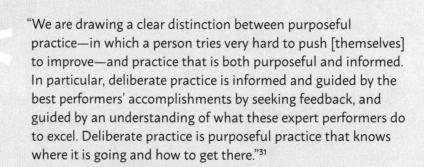

There are three different types of practices: *naive, purposeful,* and *deliberate*.[30]

- **Naive practice:** Going through the motions; repetition of the task with no goal
- **Purposeful practice:** Goal-directed, focused, includes feedback, and is challenging
- **Deliberate practice:** In addition to the aspects of purposeful practice, there is a defined expertise, and a teacher provides guidance activities and feedback

"We are drawing a clear distinction between purposeful practice—in which a person tries very hard to push [themselves] to improve—and practice that is both purposeful and informed. In particular, deliberate practice is informed and guided by the best performers' accomplishments by seeking feedback, and guided by an understanding of what these expert performers do to excel. Deliberate practice is purposeful practice that knows where it is going and how to get there."[31]

PRINCIPLES OF DELIBERATE PRACTICE

Principle	Description
Push beyond one's comfort zone	Learning is challenging work, and deliberate practice requires that students push just beyond their current abilities. Students learn to accept the challenge of learning.
Work toward well-defined, specific goals	Deliberate practice requires that efforts be aligned to specific, measurable goals that focus on a particular aspect of the skill or content rather than working toward broad general improvement.
Focus intently on practice activities	Students must learn to direct their energy and focus on meaningful tasks rather than simply trying to finish them as quickly as possible.
Receive and respond to high-quality feedback	Students seek feedback and then use that feedback in the next iteration of their effort. In doing so, they monitor their progress toward successfully meeting the goal.
Develop a mental model of expertise	Students clearly understand the skill that allows them to self-monitor and adjust their efforts.

To help students focus on the practice activities, teachers should provide **universal response opportunities** (see page 79) and vary their questioning techniques. There are three options that should be used strategically and often in the classroom when students are engaged in practice:

RANDOM SELECTION

using a tongue depressor/stick or an online name generator to identify which student(s) will share

VOLUNTEERS

inviting students to share their thinking with the group, keeping track of which students do and do not share

TEACHER CHOICE

identifying specific students, in advance, who will share

SPIDER MAP

A **spider map** is one tool for monitoring the participation in the classroom. Using a copy of the seating chart, draw lines between students as they speak. If the teacher speaks, draw a line to the teacher, then to the next student to speak, and then another line to the next person who speaks. This provides a visual of the conversation turns in the class.

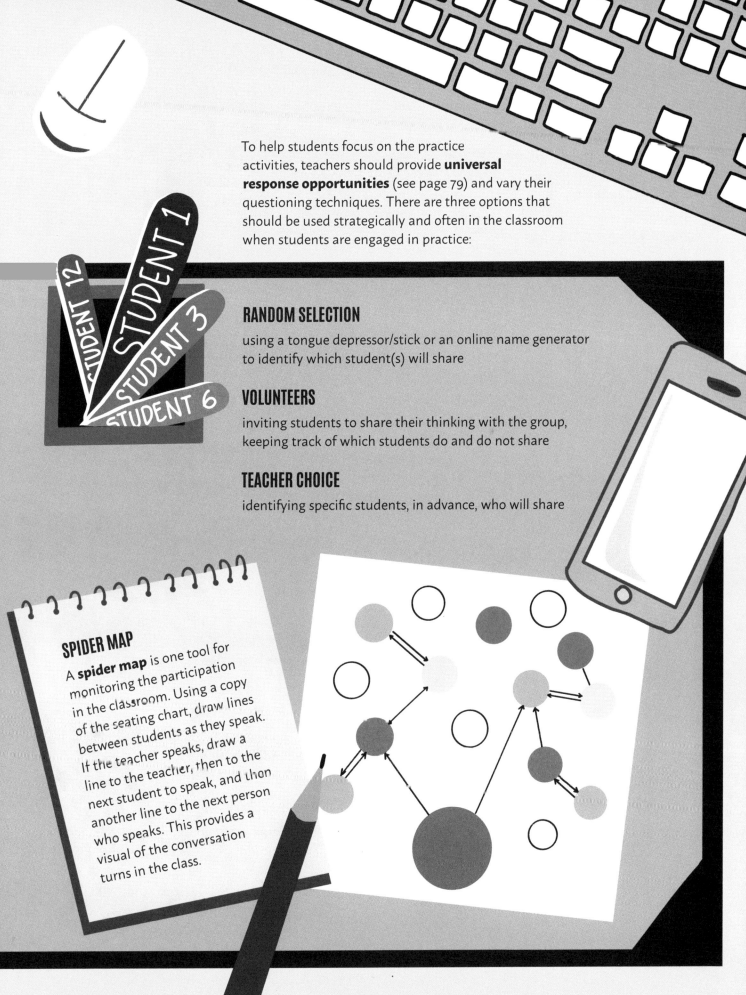

SPACED PRACTICE

Spiral review and over-learning across time are examples of spaced practice rather than mass practice. When teachers plan practice tasks for students, spacing them out over time, especially after the initial learning, it increases the likelihood that learning will occur.

Cramming, also known as massed practice, runs counter to the idea of learning. In **massed practice**, tasks are completed in time periods that are close together. Often, the information is lost if not rehearsed thereafter. Conversely, **spaced practice** is distributed and rehearsed over longer periods of time, resulting in sustained retention.

Spaced vs. mass practice

1.1
0.9
0.7
0.59
0.5
0.3
0.1
-0.1
<-0.3

Of course, we all forget things. But the **curve of forgetting** can be reduced when students practice over time.[32] Notice that the level of retention is much higher, and less forgetting occurs, with repetition of practice. The more complex the information the more students need to practice across time.[33]

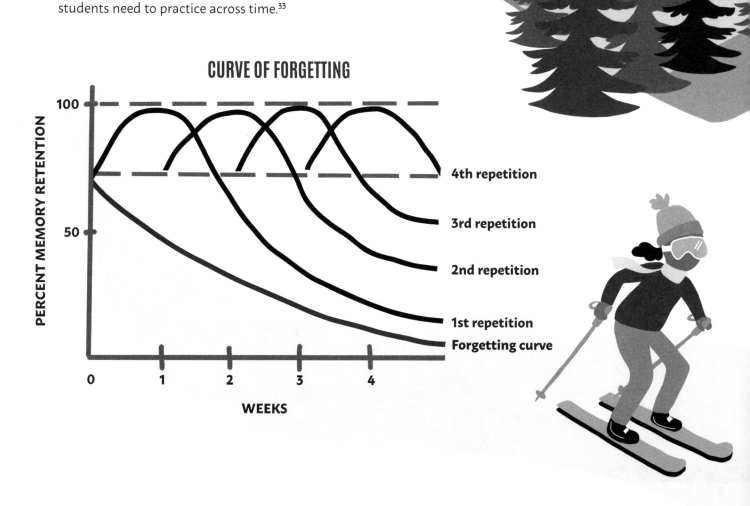

CURVE OF FORGETTING

PERCENT MEMORY RETENTION

100

50

4th repetition

3rd repetition

2nd repetition

1st repetition

Forgetting curve

0   1   2   3   4

WEEKS

Interleaved practice

0.46

Interleaved practice can also help students learn and remember things.[34] Interleaving involves mixing together different topics, subjects, ideas, skills, or forms of practice. The key is moving back and forth between the practice.

For example, solving two or more types of problems, so that you complete a small number of problems of the same type before switching to the other type of problem, and then returning to the initial set of problems.

MASSED PRACTICE

A	A	A	A

B	B	B	B

C	C	C	C

D	D	D	D

SPACED PRACTICE

A	B	B	B

A	C	C	C

A	D	D	D

A	B	C	D

INTERLEAVED PRACTICE

A	C	B	D

D	A	B	C

B	C	C	A

D	B	A	D

RETRIEVAL PRACTICE

At the most basic level, learning is about encoding information and the ability to retrieve that information. There are many ways to help students encode information, such as modeling, direct instruction, and interactive videos. But that's only part of the process. Students need to be able to recall facts, concepts, or events from memory and then use that information. There is a continual give-and-take between longer-term memory and working memory.

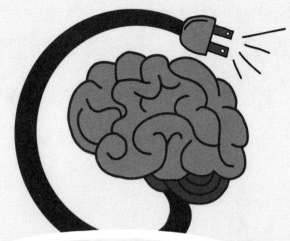

Retrieval practice is all about reconstructing the memory and reconstructing it in different ways!

RECONSOLIDATION

To **reconsolidate** the memory, students must reactivate the original memory trace. Doing so can maintain and strengthen the memory and even stabilize the knowledge in the brain.

RELEARNING

RETRIEVAL

Retrieval is part of the learning process. Retrieval allows us to use the information that we have been taught. But retrieval also facilitates **relearning** and **reconsolidation**.

Part of the learning process involves **acquisition** and **consolidation** as we learned in the section on phases of learning. But learning is more complex than that.

CONSOLIDATION

ACQUISITION

START HERE

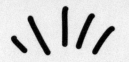

<-0.3 -0.1 0.1 0.3 0.5 0.7 0.9 1.1

0.54

Universal response opportunities are one way to encourage retrieval practice. Students all respond at the same time to a task or prompt, which also allows the teacher to check for understanding. Common universal response opportunities include

Response cards of pre-printed answers (yes/no, true/false) allow for quick checks.

Whiteboards for students allow them to write and hold up their answers.

Nonverbal hand signals give you a way to conduct a quick check. Ask students to hold their hand signal close to their chest so you can see, but others can't.

Digital polls are great for checking understanding. After answering, ask students to explain to a neighbor why they chose the answer, then ask it again. **HINT:** *turn off functions that award points based on response time.*

Four corners give students a way to determine and discuss their opinions about a topic. Post opinions in the four corners of your classroom.

VL Signature Practice #7:

FEEDBACK

FEEDBACK

Learning is fueled by feedback. The verbal and written comments created for students should represent your best thinking about how they can move forward in their learning. Feedback is not advice (*"Maybe you could add something to this part?"*), and it is not grades, which do almost nothing to influence future learning. Here are seven qualities to consider when formulating feedback.[35]

Feedback

<-0.3   -0.1   0.1   0.3   0.5   0.7   0.9   1.1

0.51

1. **Goal-referenced.** Your feedback should help students advance toward their stated learning goals.

2. **Tangible and transparent.** If they're having difficulty doing something, record it for them so they can see and hear it. This works great for disfluent readers.

3. **Actionable.** Outline next steps and give them the chance to strengthen their work.

4. **User friendly.** Don't use jargon. Make sure they can understand it.

5. **Timely.** Delayed feedback gets stale quickly, but sometimes immediate feedback makes students too dependent on you.

6. **Ongoing.** The best feedback occurs throughout the learning so that students can adjust their performance.

7. **Consistent.** Align your feedback to the rubrics, exemplars, and teacher modeling you use to explain success criteria.

8. **Future focused.** Students are improvement engines and see the value of feedback as information to help them improve.

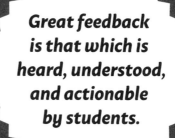

Great feedback is that which is heard, understood, and actionable by students.

The acceptance of feedback is impacted by the relationship you have with students. There are four conditions that improve the likelihood that feedback will work.

CARE

A learning atmosphere of trust and respect. When care is absent, students are guarded and may not expose their misunderstandings or be willing to accept feedback as a growth-producing event.

CREDIBILITY

The belief that the other person is worthy of listening to and learning from. Essentially, students ask themselves, "Can I learn from this person?" If the answer is yes, then feedback is much more likely to have an impact.

CLARITY

The understanding that there are things worth learning, what that learning is, and what it means to learn successfully. When these conditions are present, learners are much more likely to accept the feedback because they see it as valuable for the goals they have agreed to and desire to accomplish.

COMMUNICATION

The way in which the message is sent and whether or not learners can understand, and act on, the information shared.

Care and credibility set the foundation for **who** is giving, receiving, and integrating the feedback. Clarity sets the foundation for **what** feedback is given, received, and integrated. Communication sets the foundation for **how** the feedback is given.[36]

There are certain triggers that cause our students, and us, to disregard feedback.[37] These triggers are a natural part of being human. Recognizing potential triggers and adjusting the feedback delivered can increase the potential for the feedback to be received and integrated through the feedback loop.

1. **Identity Trigger.** Identity triggers are not about the substance of the feedback or the person delivering the feedback. Identity triggers are all about the receivers' perception of themselves. If the feedback challenges our perception of our own strengths and weaknesses or how we think about ourselves, we turn our attention to saving face and not to receiving and integrating the feedback.

2. **Truth Trigger.** If the feedback given to us is perceived as untrue, we will tune it out. A truth trigger can occur because our belief about the process or product is different from that of the person giving the feedback or as a result of the giver of the feedback not knowing about some aspect of the process or product. Truth triggers are all about the substance of the feedback and have nothing to do with the person delivering the feedback.

3. **Relationship Trigger.** Relationship triggers have all to do with who is giving the feedback. If the person giving and the person receiving the feedback do not have a strong relationship, the feedback will probably not be used to make change.

TYPES OF FEEDBACK

There are at least four types of feedback that teachers can give to students.[38] Note that some are more effective than others and that they can be combined to increase students' learning. Also note that you can praise students, but the praise should be specific. Although students deserve praise, it does not directly impact future learning.

Level of Feedback	Example	Level of Effectiveness
About the task *(corrective feedback)*	"You answered the first and third questions correctly. The second question isn't right and you might want to re-read section 2."	Effective for feedback about mistakes, learning facts and ideas, and building knowledge.
About the processing of the task	"I can see that you're graphing data to analyze it. That seems to be working well for you."	Very effective, as it labels cognitive and metacognitive strategies the learner is using or should be using.
About self-regulation	"I saw you were frustrated when you got it wrong, and I noticed that you reviewed the task sheet and found your error."	Very effective, as it helps learners to self-assess their ability, actions, and knowledge.
About the person	"Well done."	Ineffective, because it doesn't yield task-specific information.

HINT:

One of the best ways to ensure that feedback is effective is to teach students to seek out feedback. You can model seeking feedback from your students and have them use their success criteria to ask for feedback. Ask them about what they understood from your feedback, and how they could use it. If they can't answer these two questions, then the feedback is unlikely to have an impact.

If a tree falls in a forest and no one is near, does it make a noise? If feedback is given in a class, and no one hears or understands it, is it of value?

The evidence on feedback has been divided into several areas to better explain the impact of each.

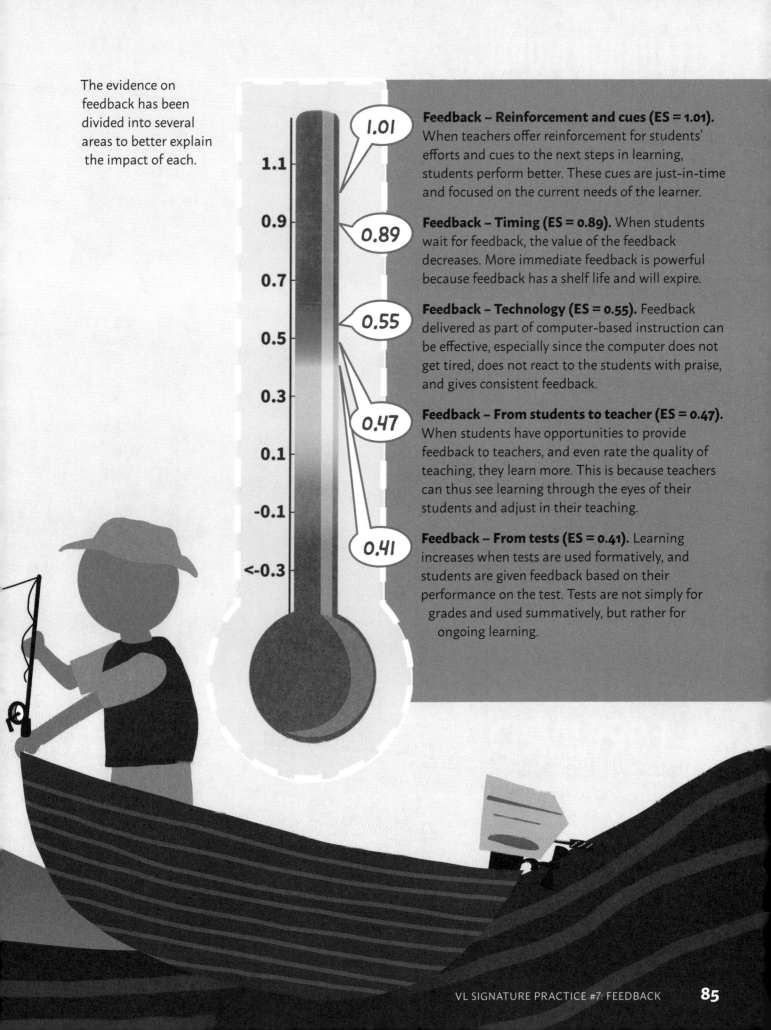

Feedback – Reinforcement and cues (ES = 1.01). When teachers offer reinforcement for students' efforts and cues to the next steps in learning, students perform better. These cues are just-in-time and focused on the current needs of the learner.

Feedback – Timing (ES = 0.89). When students wait for feedback, the value of the feedback decreases. More immediate feedback is powerful because feedback has a shelf life and will expire.

Feedback – Technology (ES = 0.55). Feedback delivered as part of computer-based instruction can be effective, especially since the computer does not get tired, does not react to the students with praise, and gives consistent feedback.

Feedback – From students to teacher (ES = 0.47). When students have opportunities to provide feedback to teachers, and even rate the quality of teaching, they learn more. This is because teachers can thus see learning through the eyes of their students and adjust in their teaching.

Feedback – From tests (ES = 0.41). Learning increases when tests are used formatively, and students are given feedback based on their performance on the test. Tests are not simply for grades and used summatively, but rather for ongoing learning.

A FEEDBACK MODEL

FEEDBACK AS A CONTINUOUS LOOP

FEED UP

Where am I going?

What is my goal?
What am I trying to achieve?

Feed up is about that first question: *Where am I going?* What is the learning intention? What is the learner trying to achieve? If our goal is to help students close the gap between where they are and where we want them to be, feedback will not lead to closing the gap if the goal is undefined because the gap will not be clear to students. Therefore, they won't see a reason to attempt to reduce it. So first and foremost, we must establish the goal, and learners need to be clear on what that goal is.

FEED FORWARD

Where to next?

What specific actions do I need to take to reduce the gap between my goal and my current level of performance?

Feed forward helps us with the question: *Where to next?* Or, how do I close the gap? What specific actions do I need to take to reduce the gap between my goal and my current level of performance?

FEED BACK

How am I going? or Where am I now?

What is my current level of performance in relation to my goal?

Feedback really answers that second question: ***How is the learner performing in relation to the goal?*** This is where success criteria are important in helping both the teacher and the student monitor progress in relation to the goal.

This feedback can come in many different forms:

1 It can give more information about what is understood or not understood.

2 It can give suggestions for more strategies or processes to utilize to complete tasks.

3 It can be aimed at increasing student fluency or automaticity, or it can give enhanced challenges to push learners to deeper understanding.

THE ILLUSTRATED GUIDE TO VISIBLE LEARNING

VL Signature Practice #8:

THE POWER OF THE COLLECTIVE

THE POWER OF THE COLLECTIVE

Collective efficacy is "a group's shared confidence and belief in the conjoint capabilities to organize and execute the courses of action required to produce given levels of attainment."[39] This applies to groups of students, educators, and leaders.

There is a reciprocal relationship between individual and collective efficacy. As one gets stronger, so does the other. Strong collective efficacy seems to encourage individual teachers to make more effective use of the skills they already have. And strong individual efficacy allows teams to function more productively.[40]

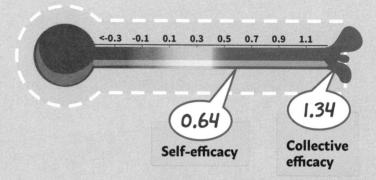

| <-0.3 | -0.1 | 0.1 | 0.3 | 0.5 | 0.7 | 0.9 | 1.1 |

0.64
Self-efficacy

1.34
Collective efficacy

The dimensions of collective efficacy are:[42, 43]

1. **Experiences of mastery** are the single most important factor in developing and reinforcing efficacy. When we experience success, we begin to attribute those successes to our actions rather than outside forces. Success breeds success. We look for situations where we believe we will succeed because it reinforces our self-efficacy.

2. **Modeling.** When we see others succeed, especially when we perceive them to be about the same as ourselves, our self-efficacy increases. To a large extent, people say to themselves, "If they can do it, so can I." Modeling experiences provide us with examples of what is possible.

3. **Social Persuasion.** Encouragement from others builds self-efficacy. We can increase our self-efficacy when we trust the person who encourages us. If the person is honest with us and we believe that that person has our best interests at heart, social persuasion can serve as a tipping point.

COLLECTIVE EFFICACY

IMPACT

4. Physiological Factors. When we experience stress, our self-efficacy is generally reduced. When we are frightened, it's hard to maintain self-efficacy. Instead, we move into a flight, fight, or freeze situation. People with higher levels of self-efficacy recognize these physiological factors and understand that they are natural biological responses to situations that do not necessarily signal failure.

5. Imaginal Experiences. The art of visualizing yourself behaving effectively or successfully in a given situation. This involves imagining you are capable of achieving what you intend to. To enhance self-efficacy, the focus needs to be on painting a picture that success seems the most likely outcome. In other words, it's seeing yourself at the finish line and believing that you can get there. [44]

6. Evidence of Impact. Success breeds success and as students make progress they are motivated to make even greater progress. When this feedback of progress is shared with others, it has a multiplying power providing energy, direction, and sustenance for all members of the collective.

EFFICACY IS FUELED BY TEACHER CREDIBILITY

At the basic level, teacher credibility is the students' perception that they will learn from this adult. The adult is seen as believable, convincing, and capable of persuading students that they can be successful. Students know which teachers can make a difference, and this can fluctuate. "The dynamic of teacher credibility is always at play."[45] There are four components of teacher credibility outlined in the research: **trust**, **competence**, **dynamism**, and **immediacy**.

TRUST

Students need to know that their teachers care about them and have their best academic and social interests at heart. Students also want to know that their teachers are reliable and true to their word. A few points about trust:

1. If you make a promise, work to keep it (or explain why you could not).

2. Tell students the truth about their performance. (They know when their work is below standard and will wonder why you are telling them otherwise).

3. Don't spend all your time trying to catch students in the wrong (and yet, be honest about their behavior's impact on you as an individual).

4. Examine your negative feelings about specific students. (They sense these feelings, and this compromises the trust within the classroom.)

COMPETENCE

In addition to trust, students want to know that their teachers know their stuff and how to teach it. They expect an appropriate level of expertise and accuracy from their teachers. Further, students measure competence by the teacher's ability to deliver coherent and organized instruction. They expect that lessons are well-paced and the information is accurate.

1. Make sure you know the content well and be honest when a question arises that you are not sure about.

2. Organize lesson delivery cohesively and coherently.

3. Consider your non-verbal behaviors that communicate competence, such as the position of your hands when you talk with students or the facial expressions you make. (Students notice defensive positions, and nonverbal indications that they are not valued when they speak.)

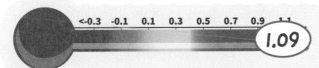

Teacher credibility

<-0.3 -0.1 0.1 0.3 0.5 0.7 0.9 1.1

1.09

When a teacher is not perceived as credible, students tune out. When teachers are credible, students engage, trust their teachers, and choose to participate in their learning.

DYNAMISM

This dimension of teacher credibility focuses on teachers' passion for the classroom and their content. It is really about the ability to communicate your enthusiasm for your subject and your students; and it's about developing spirited lessons that capture students' interest. To improve dynamism:

1. Rekindle your passion for the content you teach by focusing on the aspects that excited you as a student. Remember why you wanted to be a teacher and the content you wanted to introduce to your students. Students notice when their teachers are bored by the content and aren't interested in the topic. We think that a teacher's motto should be: make content interesting or share your passion!

2. Consider the relevance of your lessons. Does the content lend itself to application outside the classroom? Do students have opportunities to learn about themselves and their problem solving? Does the content help them become civic-minded and engaged in the community? Does it connect to universal human experiences, or ask students to grapple with ethical concerns? When there isn't relevance, students check out, and may be compliant learners rather than committed learners.

3. Seek feedback from trusted colleagues about your lesson delivery. Ask peers to focus on the energy you bring to the lesson and the impact of those lessons, rather than the individual instructional strategies you use. Students respond to the passion and energy in a lesson, even if they didn't initially think they would be interested.

IMMEDIACY

This final construct of teacher credibility focuses on accessibility and relatability as perceived by students. Teachers who move around the room and are easy to interact with increase students' perception of immediacy. Teachers need to be accessible, and yet there needs to be a sense of urgency signaling to students that their learning is important.

1. Get to know something personal about each student, as students know when you don't know their names or anything about them.

2. Teach with urgency but not to the point that it causes undue stress for them. Students want to know that their learning matters and that you are not wasting their time.

3. Start the class on time and use every minute wisely. This means that there are tasks students can complete while you engage in routine tasks such as taking attendance and that you have a series of sponge activities ready when lessons run short. Students notice when time is wasted. And when there is "free time" they believe that their learning is not an urgent consideration of their teachers.

SKILLS FOR INDIVIDUAL AND COLLECTIVE EFFICACY

To build individual and collective efficacy, there are specific skills that need to be taught and developed. Students and educators can develop both individual and collective efficacy, and when they do, they tend to perform better. We have grouped the skills necessary into the "**I**" and "**We**" skills.[46]

The "I" skills are based on self-efficacy, which includes the confidence to undertake a task. "I" skills are dependent on the Goldilocks principle: not too much and not too little confidence. Those with an abundance of confidence often underperform because they are resistant to the ideas of others and believe that their path is the only correct one. Those under-confident doubt that they possess the internal resources such as ability and perseverance and question the usefulness of external resources to complete the task. Individuals with a well-calibrated, "just right" level of self-confidence are socially aware of others, but don't spend much time in social comparisons.

"I" SKILLS

- A "just right" level of self-confidence in my own ability to contribute to the group
- Working together while following directions and delegating tasks
- Identifying challenges and overcoming obstacles

- Nonverbal communication skills (eye contact, gestures, body language, facial expressions, tone)
- Verbal communication skills (conflict resolution, negotiation, desirable argumentation)
- Seeing myself as a learner
- Setting group goals

There are many skills, or lack thereof, that can cause barriers to success in groups, including social loafing, not agreeing to rules of conduct, not establishing individual accountability, not encouraging group loyalty, not evaluating progress, and not dealing with conflict, non-participation, withdrawal, scapegoating, bullying, irregular attendance, aggressive behavior, or arguments.

When individuals develop the ability to acknowledge mistakes, accept others as they are, decode and understand what others are thinking and feeling, become social problem solvers, empathize with others and the group's moods and feelings, and listen and demonstrate they have listened to others in the group, social cohesion develops and the group is stronger.

"WE"

"WE" SKILLS

- Social sensitivity (empathy, acknowledging mistakes, accepting others)
- Motivation to tackle the task together
- Ability to take turns
- Flexibility in taking on roles within the group or team
- Determination to succeed together

- Great listeners can stand in the shoes of others
- Collective responsibility for keeping going and meeting deadlines
- A sense of group responsibility for each other as equal participants
- Being able to give supportive feedback to each other without diminishing self-efficacy

PLC+ BUILDS COLLECTIVE EFFICACY

When groups of educators come together with the belief that they have the skills to make a difference in students' lives and are fed with evidence of their impact, collective efficacy grows. A process for accomplishing this is PLC+, and updated versions of professional learning communities that have existed since the 1960s. The goal remains the same as was identified in learning-enriched schools: "improvement of teaching is a collective rather than individual enterprise, and that analysis, evaluation, and experimentation in concert with colleagues are conditions under which teachers improve."[47]

For PLCs to be effective and build collective efficacy, team members need to embrace core beliefs such as:

- We have a relentless focus on our impact on each student's learning.
- Sustained improvement requires a collective effort.
- We need to critically interpret the data together to enhance our impact.
- We will accept the difficult facts and act on them.
- We need each other to truly address the needs of all our students.

The **five guiding questions** (facing page, above) drive the investigation cycle, and **four cross-cutting values** are the focus of the process:

EQUITY

Information is processed to identify and apply appropriate and impactful evidence-based instructional practices and culturally responsive teaching that values the background of every student and helps prepare each of them for success. Valuing the assets each learner brings to the classroom requires ensuring instruction, curriculum, and assessment are responsive and affirming.

HIGH EXPECTATIONS

PLC+ teams manifest high expectations teaching by ensuring that grade-level and course standards are taught. This requires not only holding all students accountable for reaching mastery, but also holding ourselves accountable for teaching with high expectations.

Newer models of the professional learning community are driven by a series of questions that lead each investigation cycle:[48]

Where are we going?

Where are we now?

Who benefited from our efforts, and who did not?

What did we learn today?

How do we move learning forward?

Questions lead to thinking and reflecting; thinking and reflecting activate action.

However, these actions must reflect the values of our school and classrooms. These values act as guides for evaluating our decisions. Our decisions should promote equity of access and opportunity to the highest level of learning possible. Our decisions should communicate high expectations for us and our learners. Our decisions should move to promote individual and collective efficacy. And, finally, our decisions should activate the thinking and reflecting of others.

INDIVIDUAL AND COLLECTIVE EFFICACY

We can capitalize on an incredible amount of brain power when we take our individual capacity and contribute it to a collective whole. This model asks us to use our collective efficacy to create the belief that we can make an impact on each and every one of our students and align our beliefs with actions to make it so.

ACTIVATION

High functioning PLC+ teams don't just happen by chance. They require deliberate efforts and structures put in place to ensure they are efficient and focused. This requires skilled facilitation as well as participation. The team relies on all its members' growing ability to activate others' thinking and action.

VL Signature Practice #9:

LEADING LEARNING

LEADING LEARNING

While teachers have a high impact on students' learning, leaders have much to contribute to the learning lives of students across the school. Their greatest impact is on the quality of the climate and culture across the school, in the staffroom, and in EVERY class within the school.

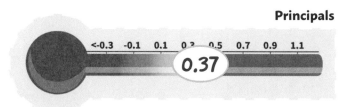

Principals

<-0.3 -0.1 0.1 0.3 0.5 0.7 0.9 1.1

0.37

CHARACTERISTICS OF LEADER CREDIBILITY

TRUST

When trust exists, things go faster.[50] It greases the wheels, so to speak. And when it's absent, people operate in fear or caution. Thus, strong leaders work to establish trust with the people they work with and among people who work together. Staff members ask, do you have my best interests at heart? Are you truthful and reliable? And do you apologize and then explain when things go wrong, making amends whenever possible? Remember, trust is easier to gain than regain.

COMPETENCE

Being seen as not knowing what you're doing compromises the impact that leaders have. People want to know that their leader has the skills to address the needs and situations that arise. The vast majority of teachers have not been principals (or coaches or even department chairs); thus, there is less clarity about the skills needed to do the job. So, a leader's competence is judged by communication skills. Staff members ask, do you have the skills to make the hard decisions, take responsibility, and develop systems that work? Are you an effective communicator, and do I know how to access you when I need to?

What leaders do and where they spend time has a powerful influence on the overall achievement of the students in their schools. Some of the different tasks that leaders do contribute to the learning of students[49]:

- Leading teacher learning and development **(ES = 0.84)**
- Establishing goals and expectations **(ES = 0.42)**
- Ensuring quality teaching **(ES = 0.42)**
- Resourcing strategically **(ES = 0.31)**
- Ensuring a safe and orderly learning environment **(ES = 0.27)**

It's hard to move learning forward in a school or system without credibility. Importantly, we did not say charisma or charm, which can have reduced impacts on teachers and students. Credibility is an accelerator of change and opens the door to coaching and feedback. Like teacher credibility, **leader credibility** has five major components.

DYNAMISM

People who exhibit dynamism are confident and they choose to engage; they are not passive participants. People want to feel important, and know that their contributions to the organization are valued. We all respond better to leaders who are dynamic in their interactions and passionate about students, student learning, and staff well-being. Educators ask, are you passionate about our school, our students, me and my development? As a leader, are you dynamic in your ideas and information presentations?

IMMEDIACY

This is about being there. Being present, both physically and mentally. Staff members wonder if they are connected with the leader. It's about relatedness and a sense of belonging that make a difference in this dimension. Staff members look for verbal and nonverbal signals that they are valued and that their voice is heard. Staff members ask, do I feel connected with you? Do I see you around the campus and are you accessible to me?

FORWARD THINKING

Credible leaders know where they are going. They have a vision, shared with school community members, that includes plans and steps for getting there. Leaders contribute the sense of a positive future, even if they do not establish all the goals and metrics for success. Instead, leaders focus on the future and help everyone see how their work contributes to the success that we all have. Educators want to be part of an organization that is mission driven, goal oriented, and well prepared for the challenges ahead—especially when they relate to enhancing the learning lives of all in the school.

SCHOOL CLIMATE

Credible leaders establish, maintain, repair, and revitalize the climate of the school. School climate refers to the social and environmental conditions that allow students to feel invited, to explore, to reach aspirations, and to learn about themselves and others.

Although the terms *school culture* and *school climate* are sometimes used interchangeably, they are related but not synonymous. **School culture** is what you do; it is the way things work in a school, including rules, procedures, and so on. But **school climate** is how it *feels*. These perceptions are likely to differ between individuals. When the school climate is positive, students learn more.

Like teachers, school leaders can find themselves on the continua of intentionality and invitation. The interactions leaders have with teachers, both the strong ones and those who need more guidance and support, set the climate for the school. Intentionality about inviting teachers to become members of the school community sets an important tone that has a ripple effect across students and families. If we want to develop caring educators, they need to know they are cared for and cared about.

INTENTIONALITY OF LEADERSHIP[51]

Intentionally Uninviting Leaders	Intentionally Inviting Leaders
• Are judgmental and belittling • Display little care or regard • Are uninterested in the lives or feelings of teachers • Isolate themselves from school life • Seek power over teachers	• Are consistent and steady with teachers • Notice learning and struggle • Respond with regular feedback • Seek to build, maintain, and repair relationships
Unintentionally Uninviting Leaders	**Unintentionally Inviting Leaders**
• Distance themselves from teachers • Have low expectations for teachers • Don't feel effective and blame teachers for shortcomings • Fail to notice when teachers learn or struggle • Offer little feedback to teachers	• Are eager but unreflective • Are energetic but rigid when facing problems • Are unaware of what works in their practice and why • Have fewer means for responding when teacher learning is resistant to their usual methods

A positive school climate is one where students feel physically and psychologically safe, where they feel that they belong, and where they are busy with the business of learning. An emotionally safe school environment is foundational; learning in a place that feels threatening is nearly impossible. Trust and belonging form the core of an emotionally safe environment. Effective schools foster a web of relationships among and between students and staff so that no one feels alone or unsupported. This web of relationships is called **social capital**. The four characteristics of social capital are:[52]

 The normative behaviors of the school (how problems are resolved and decisions are made)

 Relational networks (the triangle of interpersonal relationships between teachers, students, and their families)

 Trust in parents (the belief of school staff that parents and teachers work together effectively to achieve goals)

 Trust in students (the belief of school staff that students collaborate with teachers effectively to achieve goals)

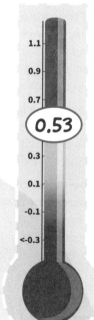

School climate

1.1
0.9
0.7
0.53
0.3
0.1
-0.1
<-0.3

There are indicators that suggest the perception of teachers, students, and parents about the climate.[53]

- Teachers in this school have frequent contact with parents.
- Parental involvement supports learning here.
- Community involvement facilitates learning here.
- Parents in this school are reliable in their commitments.
- Teachers in this school trust the parents.
- Teachers in this school trust their students.
- Students in this school can be counted on to do their work.
- Students are caring toward one another.
- Parents of students in this school encourage good schooling habits.
- Students respect others who get good grades.
- The learning environment here is orderly and focused on accelerating learning.

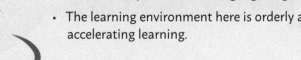

PROFESSIONAL LEARNING, COACHING, AND SUPPORT

As lifelong learners, teachers are expected to continue learning across their careers. There are many ways to provide these learning experiences and thousands of studies about professional learning. There seem to be some very effective professional learning programs, and some that are not worth the time.

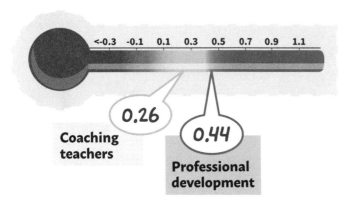

Coaching teachers 0.26

Professional development 0.44

Professional learning programs that are effective tend to have key characteristics:[54]

- **Extended time for opportunities to learn is necessary but not sufficient.** Between six months and two years are common timeframes for professional learning, especially when substantive new learning is required.

- **External expertise is typically necessary but not sufficient.** External experts bring evidence-based practices to schools, allowing for synthesis and implementation of ideas.

- **At some point, teachers' engagement in learning is more important than initial volunteering.** It does not seem to matter if participation is voluntary or compulsory. What matters is the content quality and the learning activities to support it.

- **Prevailing discourses challenged.** When teachers are challenged to consider their impact on students, including students who had experienced failure, the outcomes tend to be positive.

- **Opportunities to participate in a professional community of practice are more important than place.** On-site and off-site professional learning events seem to garner similar impacts, but when the events focus on analyzing the impact of teaching on student learning, the results are generally positive.

- **Using assessment to focus teaching and review effectiveness.** Evidence from students and the relationship between teaching and learning are important aspects of professional learning that make a difference in student achievement.

- **Active school leadership.** Effective leaders support teachers' professional learning and participate in the learning events themselves.

ADVICE

Acquiring knowledge and skills is one thing but incorporating them into practice is another. Coaching is intended to close the knowing-doing gap. However, there is limited evidence on the impact of coaching teachers and subsequent increases in student learning. That may be because leaders focus too much on advice and not as much on coaching.

Advice is one person telling another what the other should do.

Coaching is one person helping the other come up with the other's own answers and implementing teaching with the desired impact.

COACHING for IMPACT

The **Coaching for Impact** model describes three aspects of the experience that must be in place:

COACHING DISPOSITIONS
Effective habits of thinking and doing

be curious
be generous
be open

COLLABORATIVE PROCESSES
Build safe, trusting, active partnerships

trust, communication, respect, and credibility

COACHING SKILLS
Effective use of

questioning
listening
paraphrasing
reflecting

DECIDE →	CLARIFY →	GENERATE →	FOLLOW UP
Is this a coachable moment?	**What are the factors involved?**	**What are the options for action?**	**How will we follow up on our action?**
Determine whether to pursue a coaching conversation. Establish a connection to the person and the issue to be discussed.	Encourage the person to tell their story; get a clear picture of what is happening, what the "need" is, what's been tried so far, and what the effects have been.	Focus on the desired outcome—the goal—and co-create options the person could pursue to achieve their goal. Prioritize a course of action.	Reconnect with the person. Discuss the action taken. Be curious about what's next.

COACHING DISPOSITIONS

Be curious, eager to know or learn something, willing to suspend judgment and be in a state of questioning to learn more. Don't jump to the "fix it" process too quickly.

Be generous with your time, empathy, expertise, and experience. Understand the "right" balance of giving and "asking for" in a conversation.

Be open in your purpose and actions. There is clarity in what you want to achieve, why, and how you will do this. There is flexibility to engage with new or different ideas.

COACHING SKILLS

LISTENING
Active and attentive listening are crucial in a coachable conversation as what the coachee says will dictate what you will say or ask next.

ATTENTIVE LISTENING
Listening and inviting the coachee to share more, allowing the coachee more time to speak.

> *When you are listening, you are coaching; you are building trust. We all seek to be understood by others. Listening is a skill that supports this, but it needs to be mastered.*

PARAPHRASING

Paraphrasing (repeating what you hear in a different form) or reflecting (repeating what you hear exactly) support active listening and acknowledge the coachee's communication—a strong trust builder. Both show that you are listening and help the coachees understand what they say. In addition, paraphrase can help to focus and clarify by reducing a long sentence or idea to its key points.

QUESTIONING

Listening and questioning go hand in glove in the world of coaching. You first listen in order to ask the right questions to move the coachees (and the learning) forward. We need to ask questions that don't necessarily lead them where we want them to go, but to the place where the coaches can learn more about themselves or the learning need of their students. The best questions start with what, how, and when. Why questions can be useful, but they can lead to evaluations and judgment, which can close down conversations.

ACTIVE LISTENING

Listening to the spaces behind the words, listening to the silences, prompting the coachee to explore ideas, clarifying and reflecting where appropriate.

VL Signature Practice #10:
IMPLEMENTATION

IMPLEMENTATION

The various influences identified in the Visible Learning database have the potential to work. But they must be implemented to influence student learning. What determines the impact on student learning is how high-probability interventions and strategies are integrated into schools and classrooms. The implementation needs to be purposeful, intentional, and deliberately designed. We have listed several high-probability interventions and strategies throughout this guide that could be implemented.

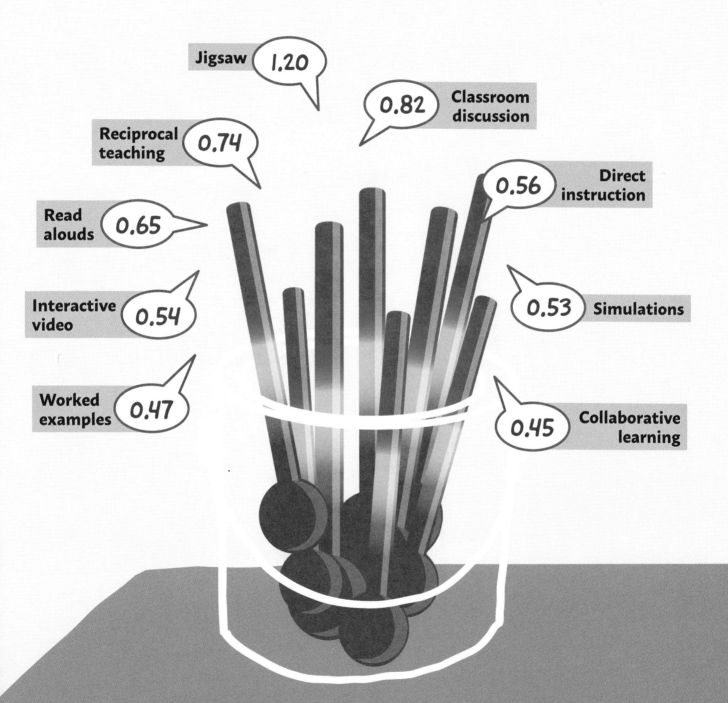

KEY ELEMENTS OF SUCCESSFUL INTEGRATION OF WHAT WORKS BEST

The **5 D model** includes[55]

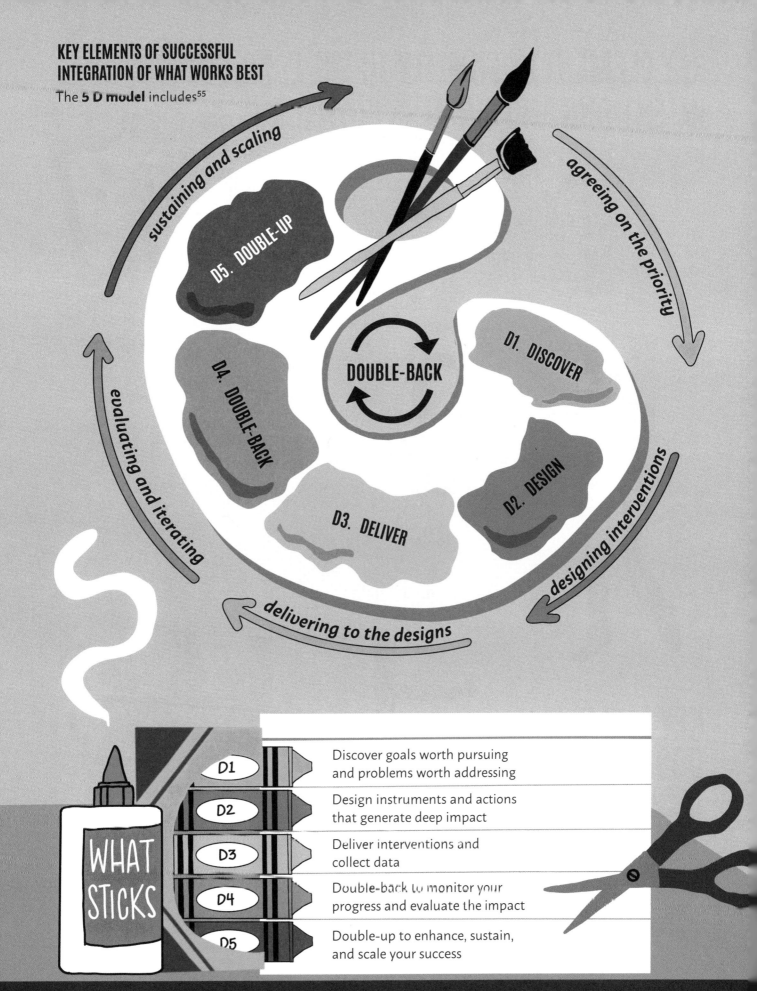

sustaining and scaling

agreeing on the priority

evaluating and iterating

designing interventions

delivering to the designs

D5. DOUBLE-UP

D4. DOUBLE-BACK

DOUBLE-BACK

D1. DISCOVER

D2. DESIGN

D3. DELIVER

WHAT STICKS

D1	Discover goals worth pursuing and problems worth addressing
D2	Design instruments and actions that generate deep impact
D3	Deliver interventions and collect data
D4	Double-back to monitor your progress and evaluate the impact
D5	Double-up to enhance, sustain, and scale your success

KEY ELEMENT 1. FIDELITY TO THE LEARNING INTENTIONS AND SUCCESS CRITERIA

The learning intentions and success criteria drive the decisions about which approaches, interventions, and strategies to select for the day's learning. Simply grabbing at any high-probability influence and dropping it into the learning experiences is gambling with student learning. This is akin to throwing spaghetti against the wall and looking to see what sticks. This is literally teaching by chance, not by design.

It is not enough for us to have clarity about learning from analyzing the standards. We must engage our learners with these learning goals. Success criteria guide the integration of high-probability interventions in three ways:

- they provide the guardrails for learners as they become aware of the success criteria and engage with the criteria to move their learning forward;

- the level of cognitive rigor, indicated by the verb, helps align the right intervention at the right time; and

- these criteria are the launch points for scaffolding learning to ensure all learners are moving toward the success criteria.

KEY ELEMENT 2. DOSAGE INCLUDES BOTH DESIGN AND DURATION

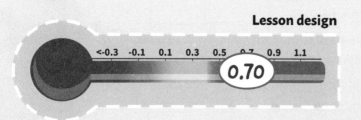

Dosage of the approach, intervention, and strategies. Dosage refers to how a particular approach, intervention, or strategy is integrated into the learning experience AND for how long. The application of this research suggests that learners persist in engaging in an experience or task when the task has clear and modeled expectations, is emotionally safe for learners to take academic risks, allows them to personalize their response, provides opportunities for choice and social interaction, and presents a novel and authentic way of seeing the content.[56]

Lesson design

<-0.3   -0.1   0.1   0.3   0.5   0.7   0.9   1.1

0.70

When designing learning experience, to ensure the proper dosage of the approach, intervention, or strategy, we must consider the following four areas of that design:[57]

FOUR COMPONENTS OF THE LESSON DESIGN

Learning Tasks	The model requires tasks that integrate skills, knowledge, and attitudes through authentic, real-life experiences. These tasks are organized from simple to complex and are scaffolded for learners. However, those scaffolds are faded out as the learners develop proficiency within the tasks.
Supportive Information	This type of information explains how learners approach the tasks (e.g., modeling, exemplars, success criteria, specific strategies, etc.).
Procedural Information	This type of information supports the learner in performing routine aspects of the experience, activity, or task. This is done through step-by-step instruction and fades away as learners develop expertise in these routine aspects (e.g., directions, instructions, guidelines, etc.).
Part-Task Practice	This component allows the learner to practice routine skills that are part of the experiences, activities, or tasks for fluency and automaticity (e.g., calculating area, identifying essential information, etc.).

Ensuring that an experience, activity, or task includes the integration of skills, knowledge, and attitudes, and that these tasks are organized from simple to complex and are scaffolded for learners, increases the potential of accelerating student learning. (Although sometimes it can be worthwhile to start with the complex to ascertain what more simple notions students may not have, work back to these, and return to the complex.)

We must know and communicate the difference between supportive and procedural information, which helps ensure learners have what they need to improve their performance in the experience, activity, or task. In the end, learners must have the opportunity to practice certain aspects of the experience, activity, or task to build fluency and automaticity with certain concepts, skills, and understandings.

What makes lesson design a powerful influence on student learning are the components of the experience, activity, or task and NOT THE COLLECTION OF EFFECT SIZES.

DOSAGE LOOK-FORS

Here are a few questions that might help ensure the proper dosage in integrating what works best into our schools, classrooms, and learning experiences:

- Do you sequence learning tasks from simple to complex?

- Do you sequence learning tasks so that the scaffolds or supports diminish over the course of the experience? We will talk more about scaffolds in just a bit.

- Do you vary the contexts of learning experiences, activities, or tasks?

- Do you present supportive information before learners begin the experience, activity, or task?

- Do you make supportive information available, if needed, during practice?

- Do you present procedural information just-in-time for learners when they need it?

KEY ELEMENT 3. ADAPTATION FOR THE SPECIFIC NEEDS OF LEARNERS

So, how do we get all learners to move toward the explicit success criteria when they enter our classrooms with such diverse characteristics, dispositions, and prior knowledge? This is what the idea of differentiated instruction has long sought to address.

But the question remains: *how to differentiate in the era of accountability?* Using instructional scaffolding, based on high expectations (i.e., learning intentions and success criteria) for all learners, helps answer that question.

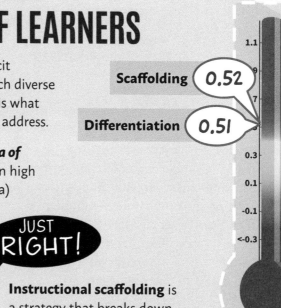

Scaffolding 0.52

Differentiation 0.51

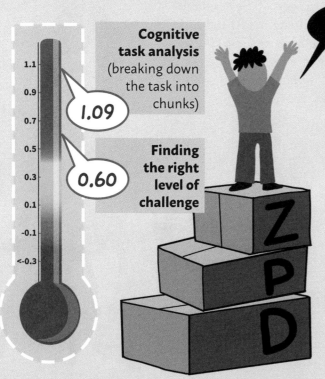

Cognitive task analysis (breaking down the task into chunks)

1.09

Finding the right level of challenge

0.60

JUST RIGHT!

Instructional scaffolding is a strategy that breaks down complex tasks into smaller, more manageable chunks, and provides the necessary supports and guidance to help students successfully engage in each of those chunks (e.g., reading *Great Expectations* or perspective drawing). Most important, any supports provided through instructional scaffolding are gradually removed as learners gain proficiency within the task and become more independent. Learning is most effective when it occurs within a student's **"zone of proximal development,"** or **ZPD**.[58] The ZPD is the area between what students can do on their own and what they can achieve with the help of a teacher or more knowledgeable other. We have referred to this concept as *the Goldilocks Principle*.

Scaffolding describes those supports, interventions, strategies, and techniques that help learners move toward meeting the learning goals in a particular learning experience or task.[59] For our exceptional learners, we would scaffold up to offer them the access and opportunity to take on a challenge, but avoid frustration, decreased motivation, and underachievement.

We propose a four-point model for adapting learning for the specific needs of learners.[60]

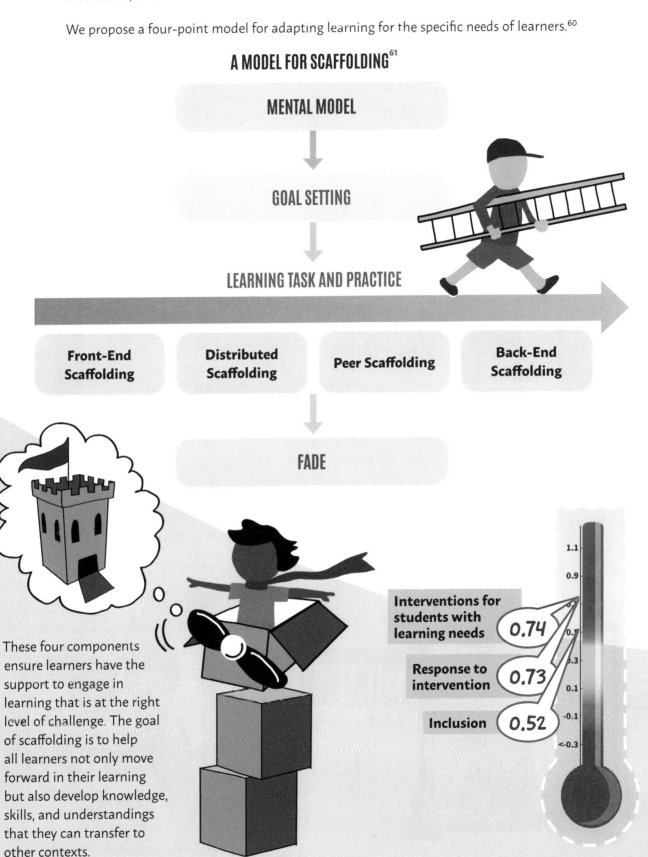

A MODEL FOR SCAFFOLDING[61]

MENTAL MODEL

↓

GOAL SETTING

↓

LEARNING TASK AND PRACTICE

| Front-End Scaffolding | Distributed Scaffolding | Peer Scaffolding | Back-End Scaffolding |

↓

FADE

These four components ensure learners have the support to engage in learning that is at the right level of challenge. The goal of scaffolding is to help all learners not only move forward in their learning but also develop knowledge, skills, and understandings that they can transfer to other contexts.

Interventions for students with learning needs **0.74**

Response to intervention **0.73**

Inclusion **0.52**

1.1
0.9
0.7
0.5
0.3
0.1
-0.1
<-0.3

KEY ELEMENT 4. QUALITY DELIVERY IN A CONDUCIVE LEARNING ENVIRONMENT

When looking at the concept of differentiation, we need to ensure there is no misunderstanding about this term. Differentiation does not mean different activities for different groups; it means different pacing and maybe different pathways for students that lead to common success criteria. If the former, there tends to be self-reinforcing expectations by students and the teacher that there will be lesser outcomes. If anything, we should think of differentiation as something that relates to differing forms of teaching, not differing forms of success.

CLASSROOM COHESION

To ignore the social-emotional aspect of integrating what works best into our schools, classrooms, and learning experiences would overlook some of the strongest factors associated with student learning. From classroom cohesion to teacher credibility, from feeling a part of the classroom community to a learner's self-efficacy, educators must recognize the unique dispositions students bring to class and create an inclusive environment that enhances their will and thrill for learning. Whether or not a learner goes along with the learning experience we design is strongly linked to our relationships with learners and the learning environment.

TEACHER-STUDENT-STUDENT RELATIONSHIPS

We must foster, nurture, and sustain a classroom culture that sees mistakes and errors as learning opportunities, encouraging teachers and learners to give and receive feedback. This cannot occur without strong, positive teacher-student and student-to-student relationships. Teacher-student relationships affect our ability to truly get to know our learners. After all, if a learner does not have a good relationship with his or her teacher, the learner may be more likely to hide mistakes and errors or take fewer risks in engaging in experiences or tasks. Without knowing our learners, we are less likely to identify, implement, and integrate an intervention that moves learning forward for that student.

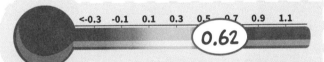

Teacher-student relationships

| <-0.3 | -0.1 | 0.1 | 0.3 | 0.5 | 0.7 | 0.9 | 1.1 |

0.62

The attributes of **warmth**, **trust**, and **empathy** lead to positive relationships:

Warmth: Warmth is demonstrated in acceptance, affection, unconditional respect, and positive regard for students. Teachers must show warmth in observable ways rather than simply intend to do so.

Trust: Students seeing that the teacher believes in them—especially when they struggle. Teachers need to have the expectation that they will be able to make it through it or that what they want to learn is worth learning.

Empathy: Teachers need to take the perspective of students if they are to get through to them. When this is understood, a teacher can know the optimal feedback to provide to move the student forward.[62]

PHYSICAL ENVIRONMENT

There is no one right way to arrange the physical environment, but there are some general guidelines that teachers can consider:

Make the space work for the interventions you plan to implement. If students need to discuss with peers, ensure the environment allows for that. If students need lab space, plan for it. If students need quiet, individual workspaces, arrange for that.

Reduce the "teacher only" space and dedicate more of the learning environment to the tasks and activities that foster learning.

Consider the walls part of the learning environment. They should not be distracting but can be used as a resource. For example, a word wall for teaching vocabulary might be useful, whereas faded motivational posters may not.

Neon bright colors should generally be avoided as they can cause tension and heighten anxiety. Generally, pastels, neutral colors, and earth tones are better.

Monitor areas or actions that cause loud noises and try to minimize the impact of the noise.

DEVELOPING AN ENVIRONMENT OF MISTAKES

As we noted earlier, educators' decisions in establishing classroom learning environments are driven by specific mindframes. An environment that allows for mistakes and errors is consistent with the mindframe: *I build relationships and trust so that learning can occur in a place where it is safe to make mistakes and learn from others.* This mindframe is paramount in creating strong, positive teacher-student relationships that allow teachers to know their learners, their learners' dispositions, unique characteristics, and where they have learning opportunities.

The following four strategies encourage the celebration of mistakes in the classroom:[63]

1. Foster the love of mistakes by talking openly about the reason they are important for learning. Not only will this bring out other learners' perspectives, but these moments are now available for all students as opportunities to learn.

2. Don't just ignore mistakes but talk about why they are important for learning. One example of this strategy is the explicit teaching of how mistakes and errors promote better learning based on how our brains encode information.

3. Demonstrate that you make mistakes, can deconstruct where and why you erred, and show the delight of learning from errors.

4. Finally, provide learners with experiences and tasks that allow for different approaches and perspectives. This opens the door to more mistakes and makes this part of the way "we do business in this class."

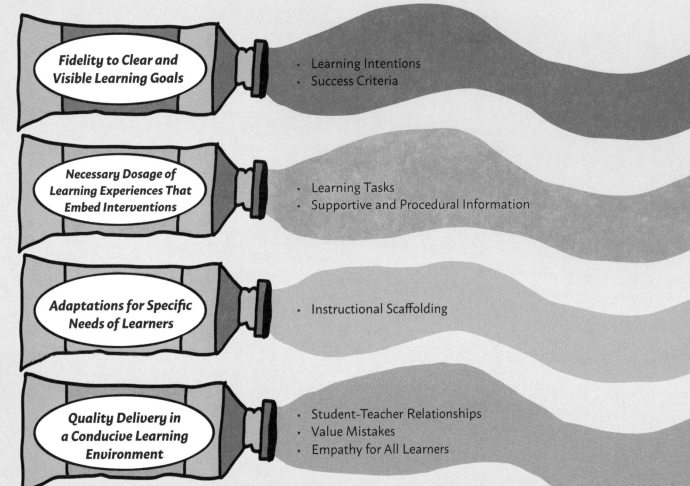

Fidelity to Clear and Visible Learning Goals
- Learning Intentions
- Success Criteria

Necessary Dosage of Learning Experiences That Embed Interventions
- Learning Tasks
- Supportive and Procedural Information

Adaptations for Specific Needs of Learners
- Instructional Scaffolding

Quality Delivery in a Conducive Learning Environment
- Student-Teacher Relationships
- Value Mistakes
- Empathy for All Learners

VL Signature Practice #11:
EVALUATIVE THINKING

EVALUATIVE THINKING

At the very start of this illustrated guide, we pointed out that while experience is a valuable teacher, it is an incomplete one. As teachers, we must make decisions based on evidence. We need to collect, interpret, and use evidence to make optimal decisions with and for students. This is a different way of thinking about our role as a teacher and our impact, through teaching, on learning. One of the most significant findings from the Visible Learning research is that it is not what we teach or how we teach, but how we think about our teaching.

As we arrive at the end of this illustrative guide for Visible Learning, we also arrive at the most significant part of our journey. Our purpose and passion, capacity and capability, ideas and impact require us to think differently about our decisions in the classroom. We must foster, nurture, and sustain evaluative thinking.

Evaluative thinking is how we move the VL Signature Practices contained in this illustrative guide from research to reality, potential to powerful practice, and from intention to integration. Evaluative thinking is how we ensure that our decisions and integration of what works best are having an impact on the learners in our classrooms.

RESEARCH

POTENTIAL

INTENTION

IMPACT

There are many different definitions of evaluative thinking. They all find different ways of capturing this form of thinking.

"Evaluative thinking is a cognitive process in the context of evaluation, motivated by an attitude of inquisitiveness and a belief in the value of evidence, that involves skills such as identifying assumptions, posing thoughtful questions, pursuing deeper understanding through reflection and perspective taking and making informed decisions in preparation for action."[65]

It is "questioning, reflecting, learning, and modifying . . . conducted all the time. It is a constant state-of-mind within an organization's culture and all its systems."[66]

"Evaluative thinking is a type of reflective practice that leads to the use of key evaluation skills in areas other than programs, strategies, and initiatives. It is an approach that fully integrates systematic questioning, data, and action into an organization's work practices."[64]

It is "an analytical way of thinking that infuses everything that goes on."[67]

to REALITY

to PRACTICE

to INTEGRATION

To tie it all together, **evaluative thinking** is:

1. **Being nosy with a reason**—the reason is knowing the impact of our decisions on student learning.

2. **Building an evidence base for learning.** We must continuously generate visible evidence that makes student thinking and learning visible. When we say we are nosy for a reason, we must have something about which to be nosy. That something is evidence of thinking and learning.

3. **Noticing.** When generating visible evidence of thinking and learning, we must recognize what we are seeing and make sense of the evidence. This is best done collaboratively with our colleagues. As we pointed out, a well-functioning PLC+ supports noticing and all other aspects of evaluative thinking.

4. **Acting.** Recognizing and making sense of the evidence generated during a learning experience is insufficient. Suppose we recognize and make sense of, say, entrance tickets, student summaries, classroom conversation, exit tickets, or other checks for understanding but simply move on to the next line of the pacing guide. In that case, we are simply asking students to engage in busy work. Instead, we must use the evidence to decide where to go "tomorrow."

QUESTIONS ASSOCIATED WITH THINKING AND ACTING EVALUATIVELY

So how can we build our capacity for evaluative thinking? How can we scaffold this way of thinking in our PLC+ teams? There are six guiding questions we can ask ourselves and our colleagues as we move away from what we teach and how we teach and toward a new way of thinking about our teaching.

These six questions are:

1. What are my learners ready to learn and what evidence supports this?

This question requires us to think evaluatively about where we are going in our teaching and their learning. This "readiness to learn" must be based on visible pre-assessment data and not on a pacing guide or "this is where we start in 4th grade." Evaluative thinking requires us to ask, **How will I know?** and asks us utilize evidence from the very start.

2. What are the potential and preferred high-probability approaches, interventions, or strategies?

Once we know what learners are ready for, do we carefully select those influences that align with the readiness (e.g., acquisition and consolidation of surface learning, acquisition and consolidation of deep learning, or transfer learning)? This aspect of evaluative thinking leads us to pick the right approach, intervention, or strategy at the right time for the right content, skill, or understanding.

IMPACT ?

3. What is the expected impact on learning and how *will* this be evaluated?

Before we get going in our teaching and learning, we must articulate our goals, outcomes, or criteria for success. What is the expected outcome of the jigsaw task, reciprocal teaching activity, or the classroom discussion on Tuesday? Plus, we must identify ways to check and see if we have had the expected impact on learning. Why are we asking them to outline and summarize? Why are we asking them to create a concept map? Why are we asking them to draw an image for each of their vocabulary words? How will we know outlining summarizing, concept mapping, and imagery worked?

4. How will the preferred evidence-based teaching interventions be integrated into the learning experience?

This question draws heavily from the VL Signature Practice focused on implementation. We must consider the different aspects of integration: 1. Fidelity to learning intentions and success criteria; 2. Dosage; 3. Adaptations for specific needs of learners; and 4. Quality delivery in an environment conducive to learning.

INTEGRATION ?

ANALYSIS

5. What happened?

During the actual learning experience, we must generate, collect, and analyze evidence of learning. This helps us answer the question about what happened during the jigsaw task, reciprocal teaching activity, or the classroom discussion on Tuesday. Do we have visible evidence of thinking and learning that allows us to see where learners are in their learning progression, where they need additional learning opportunities, and where they are ready to move forward?

INSIGHTS

6. How do I *collaborate with others* to gain insight about and improve my impact?

While we are each qualified and highly trained professionals, there is a danger in working in isolation. We often fall prey to cognitive biases that prevent us from recognizing, making sense of, and acting upon the evidence generated before, during, and after a learning experience. Some of these biases include:

Confirmation Bias: Looking for, remembering, noticing, or giving more weight to evidence that supports our already held beliefs. For example, if you believe learners struggle with a particular concept skill or understanding, you may be biased toward confirming your beliefs, ignoring evidence that says otherwise.

Bandwagon Effect: going with the flow of the crowd or not thinking independently, often based on a conscious or unconscious desire to fit in. This bias shows up in the faculty lounge, hallway, or local grocery story. For example, "Students these days just don't study." In this case, we jump on that bandwagon and focus only on evidence that aligns with that group belief.

Evaluative thinking, an essential VL Signature Practice, supports our decisions by ensuring that thinking, judgment, and action in teaching and learning are based on evidence.

This type of thinking helps us focus on what evidence we will need to collect, interpret, and use to make strong decisions with and for students. Again, it is not what we teach or how we teach, but how we think about our teaching.

"The Glass Is Half Full" Bias: This bias causes us to over-emphasize pleasing outcomes, while failing to identify limitations and weaknesses. We only see what students do well and ignore their areas for growth. We move on, believing they are ready for the next level of the progression and overlook gaps in their current knowledge, skill set, and/or understandings. While this level of optimism is refreshing, this bias can cause significant challenges as learning becomes more complex and difficult.

Appeal to Novelty Fallacy: In this situation, we prematurely approve of an approach, intervention, or strategy simply because it is new and modern. For example, we use clickers or another piece of instructional technology and attribute learning to it because it is something different. "The students just love clickers" or "my learners think [insert any tool] is awesome and get so excited when we us it" are phrases associated with this bias. This bias can cause us to miss the fact that they generated no evidence of learning or that learning was substituted by entertainment.

CONCLUSION

Your school and classroom are both complex environments and represent an incredibly diverse context in which amazing teaching and learning happen on a daily basis. At the core of this teaching and learning are those important and special interactions between teachers and students, as well as specific concepts, skills, and understandings. Our fundamental goal is to move learning forward—fostering, nurturing, and sustaining self-regulated learners that drive their own lifelong learning. As professionals, we strive to professionally grow and develop as adult learners. What we hoped to have accomplished over the pages of this illustrative guide is provide a pathway for having the greatest impact possible on every learner we encounter. We have sought to make the journey from research to practice visible to us as teachers and adult learners.

Visible Learning is both the research base and a way of approaching systemwide educational improvement that ensures every student experiences great learning—not by chance, but by design. It uses evidence from research and from practice to build the capacity required for each part of our educational system to function well, both as individual components and as a collective whole. Schools that integrate signature practices that ensure they have the knowledge and understanding about what impact is being made on every student's learning and achievement are best positioned to positively influence the learning lives of its students. Our most effective school leaders and teachers are individuals who understand how to manage school and classroom systems and processes to maximize student progress and achievement. This deep and embedded understanding is the *Visible Learning Journey*!

THE ILLUSTRATED GUIDE TO VISIBLE LEARNING

ENDNOTES

INTRODUCTION

1. Mitchel, P. (2016). *From concept to classroom.* Australian Council for Educational Research. Retrieved from https://research.acer.edu.au/cgi/viewcontent .cgi?article=1009&context=professional_dev

2. Law, N., Hollins-Alexander, S., Hattie, J., & Smith, D. (2024). *Mindframes for belonging, identities, and equity.* Corwin.

VL SIGNATURE PRACTICE #1: CLASSROOM AND SCHOOL CLIMATE

3. The Education Hub. (2018). How to develop high expectation teaching. https:// theeducationhub.org.nz/how-to-develop-high-expectations-teaching/

4. Good, T. L. (1987). Two decades of research on teacher expectations: Findings and future directions. *Journal of Teacher Education, 38*(4), 32–47.

5. Cohen, G.L. (2022). *Belonging: The science of creating connection and bridging divides.* Norton.

6. Carter, E.W. (2021). Dimensions of belonging for individuals with intellectual and developmental disabilities. In J.L. Jones & K.L. Gallus (Eds.), *Belonging and resilience in individuals with developmental disabilities* (pp. 13–33). Springer Nature.

7. Evans, C.R., & Dion, K.L. (1991). Group cohesion and performance: A meta-analysis. *Small Group Research, 22,* 175–186.

8. Kleinfeld, J. (1975). Effective teachers of Eskimo and Indian students. *School Review, 83,* 301–344.

9. Rogers, C. R. (1957). The necessary and sufficient conditions of therapeutic personality change. *Journal of Consulting Psychology, 21,* 95–103.

10. Purkey, W. W., & Novak, J. M. (1996). *Inviting school success: A self-concept approach to teaching, learning, and democratic practice* (3rd ed.). Wadsworth Publishing.

11. Purkey, W. W., & Novak, J. M. (1996). *Inviting school success: A self-concept approach to teaching, learning, and democratic practice* (3rd ed.). Wadsworth Publishing.

VL SIGNATURE PRACTICE #2: TEACHER CLARITY

12. Lassiter, C., Fisher, D., Frey, N., & Smith, D. (2022). *How leadership works: A playbook for instructional leaders.* Corwin.

13. Priniski, S. J., Hecht, C. A., & Harackiewicz, J. M. (2018). Making learning personally meaningful: A new framework for relevance research. *Journal of Experimental Education, 86,* 11–29.

14. Fisher, D., Frey, N., Ortega, S., & Hattie, J. (2023). *Teaching students to drive their learning: A playbook on engagement and self-regulation.* Corwin.

15. Hattie, J.A.C., Hodis, F.A., & Kang, S.H. (2020). Theories of motivation: Integration and ways forward. *Contemporary Educational Psychology, 61,* 101865.

16. Lassiter, C., Fisher, D., Frey, N., & Smith, D. (2022). *How leadership works: A playbook for instructional leaders.* Corwin.

VL SIGNATURE PRACTICE #3: PHASES OF LEARNING

17. Hattie, J., & Donoghue, G. M. (2016). Learning strategies: A synthesis and conceptual model. *Science of Learning, 1.* doi:10.1038/npjscilearn2016 npjscilearn.2016.13.

18. Hattie, J. (2023). *Visible learning: The sequel. A synthesis of over 2,100 meta-analysis relating to achievement.* New York, NY: Routledge.

VL SIGNATURE PRACTICE #4: TEACHING STUDENTS TO DRIVE THEIR LEARNING

19. Berry, A. (2020). Disrupting to driving: Exploring upper primary teachers' perspectives on student engagement. *Teachers and Teaching, 26*(2), 145–165.

20. Fisher, D., Frey, N., Ortega, S., & Hattie, J. (2023). *Teaching students to drive their learning: A playbook on engagement and self-regulation.* Corwin.

21. Adesope, O. O., Trevisan, D. A., & Sundararajan, N. (2017). Rethinking the use of tests: A meta-analysis of practice testing. *Review of Educational Research, 87*(3), 659–701.

22. Carless, D., & Boud, D. (2018) The development of student feedback literacy: Enabling uptake of feedback. *Assessment & Evaluation in Higher Education, 43*(8), 1315–1325.

23. Frayer, D.A., Frederick, W. C., & Klausmeier, H. J. (1969). *A schema for testing the level of concept mastery (Working paper No. 16).* Madison, WI: Wisconsin Research and Development Center for Cognitive Learning.

24. Werft, S. (2019, May 15). How do you know you've learned something? Retrieved from https://www.linkedin.com/pulse/how-do-you-know-youve-learned-something-stjepan-werft/

25. Frey, N., Fisher, D., & Almarode, A. (2023). *How scaffolding works: A playbook for supporting and releasing responsibility to students.* Corwin.

VL SIGNATURE PRACTICE #5: TEACHING WITH INTENT

26. Fisher, D., & Frey, N. (2021). *Better learning through structured teaching: A framework for the gradual release of responsibility* (3rd ed.). ASCD.

27. Fisher, D., & Frey, N. (2021). *Better learning through structured teaching: A framework for the gradual release of responsibility* (3rd ed.). ASCD.

28. Fisher, D., & Frey, N. (2008). Homework and the gradual release of responsibility: Making student "responsibility" possible. *English Journal, 98*(2), 40–45.

VL SIGNATURE PRACTICE #6: PRACTICE AND OVER-LEARNING

29. Schwartz, I., & Woods, J. (2015). Making the most of learning opportunities. In Division of Early Childhood (Ed.), *DEC recommended practices: Enhancing services for young children with disabilities and their families.* Division of Early Childhood.

30. Ericsson, A., & Pool, R. (2016). *Peak: Secrets from the new science of expertise.* Houghton Mifflin Harcourt.

31. Ericsson, A., & Pool, R. (2016). *Peak: Secrets from the new science of expertise.* Houghton Mifflin Harcourt.

32. Ebbinghaus, H. (1913/1885). *Memory: A contribution to experimental psychology* (H. A. Ruger & C. E. Bussenius, trans.). New York: Teachers College, Columbia University.

33. Cepeda, N. J., Pashler, H., Vul, E., Wixted, J. T., & Rohrer, D. (2006). Distributed practice in verbal recall tasks: A review and quantitative synthesis. *Psychological Bulletin, 132*(3), 354.

34. Firth, J., Rivers, I., & Boyle, J. (2021). A systematic review of interleaving as a concept learning strategy. *Review of Education, 9*(2), 642–684.

VL SIGNATURE PRACTICE #7: FEEDBACK

35. Wiggins, G. (2012). Seven keys to effective feedback. *Educational Leadership, 70*(1), 10–16.

36. Almarode, J., Fisher, D., & Frey, N. (2023). *How feedback works: A playbook.* Corwin.

37. Stone, D., & Heen, S. (2014). *Thanks for the feedback. The science and art of receiving feedback well.* Penguin.

38. Hattie, J., & Timperley, H. (2007). The power of feedback. *Review of Educational Research, 77*(1), 81–112.

VL SIGNATURE PRACTICE #8: THE POWER OF THE COLLECTIVE

39. Bandura, A. (1997). *Self-efficacy: The exercise of control.* New York: W.H. Freeman. P. 447

40. Hoy, W.K., Sweetland, S.W., & Smith, P.A. (2002). Toward an organizational model of achievement in high schools: The significance of collective efficacy. *Education Administration Quarterly, 38*(1), 77–93.

41. Bandura, A. (2006). Guide for constructing self-efficacy scales. In F. Pajares & T. Urdan (Eds.), *Self-efficacy beliefs of adolescents* (pp. 307–337).

42. Bandura, A. (1993). Perceived self-efficacy in cognitive development and functioning. *Educational Psychologist, 28,* 117–148.

43. Maddux, J.E. (2013). *Self-efficacy, adaptation, and adjustment: Theory, research, and application.* Springer.

44. Maddux, J. E., & Meier, L. J. (1995). Self-efficacy and depression. In J.E. Maddux (Ed.), *Self-efficacy, adaptation, and adjustment* (pp. 143–169). Springer, Boston, MA.

45. Fisher, D., Frey, N., & Hattie, J. (2016). *Visible learning in literacy.* Corwin.

46. Hattie, J., Fisher, D., Frey, N., & Clarke, S. (2021). *Collective student efficacy: Developing independent and inter-dependent learners.* Corwin.

47. Rosenholtz, S. (1989). *Teacher's workplace: The social organization of schools.* Longman.

48. Fisher, D., Frey, N., Almarode, J., Flories, K., & Nagel, D. (2019a). *PLC+: Better decisions and greater impact by design.* Corwin.

VL SIGNATURE PRACTICE #9: LEADING LEARNING

49. Robinson, V. (2011). *Student-centered leadership.* Jossey-Bass.

50. Covey, S. (2008). *The speed of trust: The one thing that changes everything.* New York: Simon & Schuster.

51. Lassiter, C., Fisher, D., Frey, N., & Smith, D. (2022). *How leadership works: A playbook for instructional leaders.* Corwin.

52. Salloum, S., Goddard, R., & Larsen, R. (2017). Social capital in schools: A conceptual and empirical analysis of the equity of its distribution and relation to academic development. *Teachers College Record, 119,* 1–29.

53. Goddard, R. D. (2003). Relational networks, social trust, and norms: A social capital perspective on students' chances of academic success. *Educational Evaluation & Policy Analysis, 25*(1), 71.

54. Timperley, H., Wilson, A., Barrar, H., & Fung, I. (2007). *Teacher professional learning and development: Best evidence synthesis iteration.* New Zealand Ministry of Education.

VL SIGNATURE PRACTICE #10: IMPLEMENTATION

55. Hamilton, A., Reeves, D.R., Clinton, J.M., & Hattie, J. (2023). *Building to impact: The 5D implementation playbook for educators.* Corwin.

56. Antonetti, J., & Stice, T. (2018). *Powerful task design: Rigorous and engaging tasks to level up instruction.* Corwin.

57. Adapted from Costa, J. M., Miranda, G. L., & Melo, M. (2022). Four-component instructional design (4C/ID) model: A meta-analysis on use and effect. *Learning Environments Research, 25,* 445–463.

58. Vygotsky, L. S. (1978). *Mind in society: The development of higher psychological processes.* Harvard University Press.

59. Wood, D., Bruner, J. S., & Ross, G. (1976). The role of tutoring in problem solving. *Journal of Child Psychology and Psychiatry, 17*(2), 89–100.

60. Frey, N., Fisher, D., & Almarode, J. (2023). *How scaffolding works: A playbook for supporting and releasing responsibility to students.* Corwin.

61. Fisher, D., Frey, N., & Almarode, J. (2023). *How scaffolding works: A playbook for differentiated learning.* Corwin.

62. Cornelius-White, J. (2007). Learner-centered teacher-student relationships are effective: A meta-analysis. *Review of Educational Research, 77*(1), 113–143.

63. Boaler, J. (2016). *Mathematical mindsets: Unleashing students' potential through creative math, inspiring messages, and innovative teaching.* Jossey-Bass.

VL SIGNATURE PRACTICE #11: EVALUATIVE THINKING

64. Baker, A. & Bruner, B. (2012). *Integrating evaluative capacity into organizational practice.* The Bruner Foundation. Retrieved from: http://www.evaluativethinking.org/docs/Integ_Eval_Capacity_Final.pdf

65. Archibald, T. (2013). "Evaluative thinking." *Free Range Evaluation,* WordPress, 11 November 2013. Retrieved from: https://tgarchibald.wordpress.com/2013/11/11/18/

66. Bennett, G. & Jessani, N. (Eds). (2011). *The knowledge translation toolkit: Bridging the know-do gap: A resource for researchers.* New Delhi, India: Sage.

67. Patton, M. Q. (2005). *In conversation: Michael Quinn Patton. Interview with Lisa Waldwick, from the International Development Research Center.* Retrieved from: http://www.idrc.ca/en/ev-30442-201-1-DO_TOPIC.html

THE ILLUSTRATED GUIDE TO VISIBLE LEARNING

INDEX

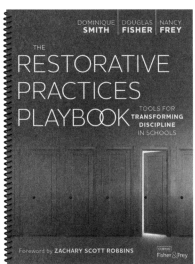

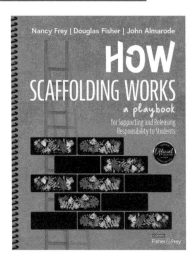

Put your learning into practice

When you're ready to take your learning deeper, begin your journey with our PD services. Our personalized professional learning workshops are designed for schools or districts who want to engage in high-quality PD with a certified consultant, measure their progress, and evaluate their impact on student learning.

CORWIN PLC+

Empower teacher teams to build collective agency and remove learning barriers

It's not enough to just build teacher agency, we must also focus on the power of the collective. Empowering your PLCs is a step toward becoming better equipped educators with greater credibility to foster successful learners.

Get started at corwin.com/plc

CORWIN Teacher Clarity

Students learn more when expectations are clear

As both a method and a mindset, Teacher Clarity allows the classroom to transform into a place where teaching is made clear. Learn how to explicitly communicate to students what they will be learning on a given day, why they're learning it, and how to know if they were successful.

Get started at corwin.com/teacherclarity

CORWIN Visible Learning+®

Translate the science of how we learn into practices for the classroom

Discover how learning works and how this translates into potential for enhancing and accelerating learning. Learn how to develop a shared language of learning and implement the science of learning in schools and classrooms.

Get started at corwin.com/visiblelearning

Experience the Corwin Difference.
Learn more at **corwin.com/the-corwin-difference**

CORWIN

FF23626467

CORWIN

A Sage Company

CORWIN HAS ONE MISSION: to enhance education through intentional professional learning.

We build long-term relationships with our authors, educators, clients, and associations who partner with us to develop and continuously improve the best evidence-based practices that establish and support lifelong learning.